Having negotiated the bottleneck of lines converging to the south of Rugby station and the scheduled stop on Saturday 22 July 1961, Stanier Coronation pacific No. 46225 DUCHESS OF GLOUCESTER works back into its stride hauling the 1.30 p.m. train from Euston to Perth. In the background are some of the railway facilities that covered a large acreage of the Midland town. The birdcage girder bridge behind Rugby Midland station carried the tracks of the old Great Central Railway over the West Coast main line.

(Michael Mensing)

A RETURN TICKET TO SCOTLAND

Part One

OUT VIA THE WEST COAST ROUTE

At a very wet Hest Bank on Friday 20 June 1958 the down 'Caledonian' races through behind Stanier Coronation pacific No. 46224 PRINCESS ALEXANDRA. (*R. Butterfield – Initial Photographs*)

Frontispiece. The magic of the Western Highlands of Scotland is seen in all its glory looking across the Inner Sound to Skye, and steam has once more returned to the Highlands in the form of Stanier 'Black 5' No. 5025. The locomotive is leaving Kyle of Lochalsh light engine for Inverness on Tuesday 5 October 1982.

(John Cooper-Smith)

A RETURN TICKET TO SCOTLAND

Part One
OUT VIA THE WEST COAST ROUTE

by

RICHARD COLEMAN and JOE RAJCZONEK

W. D. WHARTON
Wellingborough

First published in 2005 by
W. D. Wharton
37 Sheep Street
Wellingborough
Northamptonshire NN8 1BX

ISBN 1 899597 18 2

Designed and typeset by John Hardaker, Wollaston, Northamptonshire
Printed and bound in Great Britain by
Butler & Tanner Ltd.
Frome, Somerset

ACKNOWLEDGEMENTS

First and foremost we must thank all the photographers represented in the following pages without whose dedication with the camera this book would not have been possible.

In this context, we include Richard Casserley for giving us access to his father Henry's photographs, transporting glass plates many miles for printing purposes and providing much information, likewise David Cross for the use of his father Derek's images.

Brian Stephenson for Rail Archive Stephenson, Graham Stacey for the LCGB Ken Nunn collection, Barry Hoper for The Transport Treasury, Trevor Ermel of Monochrome, and Chris Leigh and Alistair Nisbet for helping us to contact a number of photographers. A big 'thank you' must also go to Colin Stacey of Initial Photographs who printed the photographs from the H. C. Casserley and W. S. Sellar collections amongst others, very often at short notice and whose patience we must have tested on several occasions and whom we also consulted as a source of reference.

Compiling information for caption writing can be very time consuming and a special 'thank you' must go to W. A. C. (Bill) Smith without whose knowledge many of the captions would be all the poorer and whom we consulted constantly. Also to others who provided information, including David Anderson and, for rolling stock details, Chris Youett and David Walker.

The foreword has been written by our old friend Neville Simms who has kindly recalled one of his many trips to Scotland in those far off days of steam traction.

Finally we would like to thank John Hardaker for his editorial advice and our publisher Robert Wharton for trusting us once more to come up with the right package.

Title page caption:
With the light fading fast, LMS 2P 4-4-0 No. 646 and Hughes Mogul 2-6-0 No. 2918 prepare to leave Stranraer Harbour station with the 9.55 p.m. boat train for Euston on Monday 21 June 1937.
(*H. C. Casserley*)

Foreword caption:
Carnforth shed was one of the last to close in August 1968 at the same time as the last steam locomotives were withdrawn from service on British Railways. Here on Sunday 26 February 1967, a railwayman takes his children to sample the unique atmosphere that existed walking amongst rows of large simmering steam locomotives, an experience that many older railway enthusiasts will remember. Stanier 'Black 5' No. 45326, a local resident, basks in the sun. (*Neville Simms*)

CONTENTS

INTRODUCTION

At the time most of the photographs in this book were taken, the only option for most people wanting to make the long trip from London to Scotland was to use the railway. A first-hand account of what this was like is given in the foreword by our photographer friend Neville Simms who describes an overnight journey in 1949 via the West Coast Main Line. The first chapter is also devoted to the route north to the border.

Once in Scotland the great diversity of railway locations is portrayed to stunning effect by a special selection of pictures from a dedicated band of photographers, whose images range from the sheer grandeur of Highland mountain scenery to the grime and smoke of Glasgow's ex-Caledonian Low Level line. We are grateful for the enthusiasm of these photographers, from Scotland and from far and wide, some of whom set out on long and uncomfortable journeys in all weathers carrying what in the early days was heavy camera equipment and as many glass plates as they could pack into their suitcase.

And in choosing from the many pictures they took, we have looked for those which are photographically artistic and which we feel best convey the feeling and atmosphere of a working railway as it was then. That is why, wherever possible, we have picked scenes that include railway personnel, passengers and onlookers going about their business, even if that involves just standing on the platform at the front of the train gazing in admiration at the steam locomotive, be it a massive pacific at one of the main line stations or a humble tank or goods engine at a wayside branch line halt.

Where available, we have included in the captions observations from the notebooks written at the time by the photographers, and also snippets from the excellent writings of H. C. Casserley, W. A. C. Smith and railway journalists C. Hamilton Ellis and O. S. Nock, all of whom have had a great affection for the railways of Scotland and who describe so well their journeyings and what they observed right through from the pre-grouping era onwards.

So join us on a trip back in time, mostly through the first sixty years of the twentieth century when life in general was harder but not so hectic and steam ruled the roost on our railway lines both north and south of the border.

Richard Coleman
Joe Rajczonek

FOREWORD

It's the summer of 1949, and the plan is to travel by overnight train to visit Scotland for the first time, destination Fort William. The choice is between the 6.55 p.m. from King's Cross and the 7.30 p.m. ex-Euston. We opt for the latter as the East Coast route will be used for our return from Edinburgh. Having saved the £7.12s.6d for the return ticket, luggage packed, along with camera, notebooks and a wad of shed permits, there is a great feeling of anticipation. Visions of lochs and mountains come to mind, not to mention the prospect of seeing some of the old pre-grouping Scottish locomotives.

Making our way through the Gothic Arch and the Great Hall at Euston one cannot help but be impressed with the grandeur of it all. Oh, those lovely red carpets. The lady announcer gives details of departures, changes en route and arrivals over the Tannoy public address system in crystal clear early BBC diction as we join the mêlée on the platform in the rush for seats. It is imperative to get window seats; you can always pretend to look out, even if there is nothing to be seen in the dark. To be in the middle, opposite someone sleeping with their mouth open for 12 hours or so, is to be avoided at all cost.

The train is a mix of sleepers and compartment stock, eight for Perth and Forfar, five for Oban, with a restaurant car bringing up the rear. This will be left behind at Crewe. At the head of the train is a rather grimy rebuilt Scot, tender stacked high with coal, and simmering from the safety valves. A discernible pull on the couplings, accompanied by the sound of escaping steam and locomotive whistles, signal that we are under way on a journey of around 526 miles. As we pick up speed I notice that the familiar rhythmic duddidy-dun of carriage wheels on rail joints is different, then realise that the peculiar syncopation is caused by being next to a sleeping carriage fitted with six-wheeled bogies.

After climbing Camden Bank and eventually leaving the city lights, the thrill of speeding into the empty blackness of the night, punctuated only by wayside stations and the oil lamps of lonely signal boxes, is quite exhilarating, but also rather soporific, and after intermittent dozing the train eventually rolls into Crewe Station, its platforms thronging with people changing trains and barrows loaded with mailbags. I lean out of the window's top light to try to catch the platform trolley in order to supplement one's overnight rations. The chance of a walk down the platform to witness the locomotive change is out of the question for fear of losing one's seat. One of Crewe North's finest locomotives is required now to lift this little lot over Grayrigg, Shap, Beattock and Gleneagles summits. Not that any great speed is required, there is no point in getting there at 4 o'clock in the morning.

We leave the station and head off once more into the blackness, passing North shed with lines of unidentifiable locomotives, and after much nodding and swaying through Wigan, Preston and Lancaster, I wake with a start. A glimpse out of the window reveals the dark shapes of the impressive Lune Valley fells against the night sky, a mental note is made to see this in daylight sometime. Soon the steady powerful pulsating beat of the Stanier pacific at the head of the train is heard as she gets to grips with the gradients ahead; music to my ears, but no one else in the compartment seems to notice. The approach to Carlisle brings the excitement of the first sighting of a real Scottish engine; 'Quentin Durward' is shunting empty stock. A touch of irony is not lost on me, the only GWR 4-6-0 I failed to see carried the same name but this 'Quentin Durward' has a painted name! Could our friends north of the border not afford nameplates? Or is it easier to correct the spelling of the Gaelic names this way? No, it's just the way they used to do them, and very smart they look too.

The next thing I know, we are slowing down on the approach to Beattock. We are in Scotland, and I have to pinch myself to really believe it. A walk to the back of the train in order to stretch one's legs and lean out of the window to try to identify the Caley 4-6-2 tank that is buffering up behind us is all in vain; it is still too dark. Several more are seen in silhouette as we pass through the station. However, if the visual is lacking, it is compensated for by the sound effects of locomotives hard at work as we are pushed up to the summit. Next time I wake up it is getting light, thank goodness, and we are approaching Stirling, gateway to the Highlands. Our coaches are detached here and our waiting Stanier Class 5 sounds more than ready, judging from the roar of steam from the safety valves. We leave the station, crossing the winding River Forth, with the Castle to the left, the Ochil Hills to the right and the Wallace Monument at the top; all very impressive. I cannot wait to see the Highlands proper. Up the hill to Dunblane, then on to the single track through Callander and we are in the mountains, gorgeous, down the Pass of Leny, along the shores of Loch Lubnaig, through the Braes of Balquhidder – Rob Roy country this – and on past Lochearnhead, situated down on the branch to Crieff. I like the light blue signs of the Scottish Region stations. Better than the drab colours of the Midland and Eastern Regions. The lattice signals and footbridges which appear to be the same over most of the country give a real Scottish feel to the stations.

As we start to climb through Glen Ogle, the view down Loch Earn is stunning. I have not heard a 'Black 5' work this hard before, as the sound of the exhaust echoes back from the mountains. The boiler, however, easily keeps pace; well done Sir William for designing such a masterpiece. As we breast the summit and head west we look down on the beautiful Loch Tay and the village of Killin. A plume of smoke in the still air is the give-away to the location of Loch Tay shed, where the Caley 0-4-4 tank is being prepared for its first trip of the day. As our train rolls into Killin junction, we see the branch trail in from the right. I lean out of the window, it is a lovely morning, the air is like wine, only the gentle hiss of steam and the greetings between station staff and footplate crew disturb the tranquillity. The station is halfway up the mountain, the nearest road is way down there, the tiny hamlet of Ardghyle, a good 20 minutes clamber down the slope. Not even a path. You want to linger in the calm of this railway oasis and see the Caley tank arrive on the branch train, but we head on down Glen Dochart to Crianlarich Lower, where we de-train, just as a 'Glen' is leaving the upper level with some sleeping cars. Looks like the First portion of the 6.55 p.m. from King's Cross. So, today 'The Race to the North' looks like a draw! Our Class 5 heads its train away towards Oban as we climb the stairs to the West Highland platform; an island platform which reminds me of stations on the Great Central Railway. What a good idea to have two water columns each end for thirsty double headers.

Our train soon arrives – looks like a relief from Glasgow – six coaches, nearly empty, hauled by a locomotive that looks like a Baby B1 and bears the name 'MacCailin Mor'. It is the K4 rebuilt into the prototype K1/1. Off we go up to the Perth/Argyll county march summit, and as we round the bends the smoke lays perfectly above the train. Oh to be on the lineside, but one cannot be in two places at once. Through the delightfully named Bridge of Orchy and on towards Gorton, the small wheels of the 2-6-0 make mincemeat of the gradients; sounds like we are doing 80 mph. I doubt if we are doing 35! At Gorton we pass a coach on the platform that is a school for railwaymen's children, and then head out onto Rannoch Moor. The mountains suddenly seem a long way away, I think we are on top of the world. A great swampy plateau with rocky outcrops – a breeding ground for midges! On reaching Rannoch station we pass a short goods train headed by a brand new locomotive. The excitement grows, it is a K1 just out of Glasgow's NBL workshops, being run-in prior to despatch to an English shed. Our own locomotive's exhaust deepens on the steepening gradient as we pound through the snow shed at Cruach Rock heading towards the summit at Corrour, and then back into the mountains. Again, the scenery defies description; Loch Treig is seen far below us, but in minutes it is level with us – a strange sensation, as we continue hurtling downhill through Tulloch and into the Monessie Gorge whose foaming waters look like ginger beer. A road has now joined us, but the Gorge is best seen from the train. All too soon we have rounded the Ben Nevis range and are down to sea level coming into Fort William. The locomotive shed, on the site of the old fort, displays some Sassenachs in the shape of ex-Great Northern Railway K2 Class 2-6-0s. These are the lifeblood of the West Highland today. We pull up in the station, the waters of Loch Linnhe almost lapping the platform. A MacBrayne steamer awaits passengers from the train, while at the adjacent platform stands a local train for Mallaig, its apple green locomotive is named 'Lord of the Isles'. What a fitting climax to an epic journey.

And so the exploration of Scotland and its railways over a number of years had begun, and in the two volumes of *A Return Ticket to Scotland* you can retrace the photographers' paths and share the sights they saw in that bygone age which they had the foresight to preserve for posterity.

Neville Simms

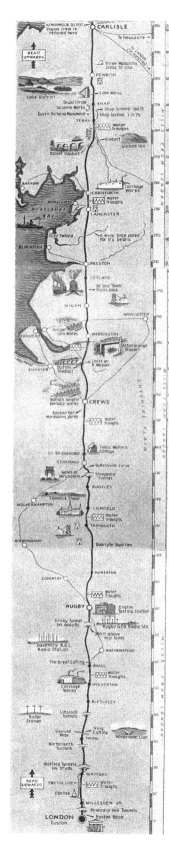

HEADING NORTH
Euston to Carlisle

1. Known as 'The Gateway to the North', Hardwick's famous Doric arch stood guard over Euston station for 123 years. This impressive entrance, which was followed by the building of the Great Hall, created a grandeur which made travellers feel that they were entering a most important station and railway. The arch is viewed here on Sunday 17 August 1947.

(W. J. S. Meredith)

2. The character of the old Euston station is personified in this scene at platforms 13 and 14 in 1948, as shafts of sunlight filter through the smoke haze onto people from all walks of life intent on reaching their respective destinations. Most will be enjoying the relaxed atmosphere after the tensions of the Second World War, although food rationing and other restrictions were still in operation. *(National Railway Museum 165/93)*

3. When William Stanier introduced his first pacific locomotive for the LMS in June 1933 it created a great deal of interest amongst the press and travelling public as well as the railway aficionados. Here at Euston station a short time exposure captures the scene as No. 6200 THE PRINCESS ROYAL, allocated to Camden shed, simmers at platform 2 after arriving with the up 'Royal Scot' in the year of its construction. On the platform men and boys inspect 6200 whilst savouring the unique aromas of hot oil, steam and smoke that emanate from a steam locomotive, particularly after a long fast run.

4. Ever the railway enthusiast, Henry Casserley cannot help glancing across to see what is going on as he and his new bride pose for the camera at Euston alongside the immaculately turned out Royal Scot No. 6115 SCOTS GUARDSMAN. The locomotive is simmering at the head of 'The Royal Highlander', an overnight sleeping car train on which they would be heading towards Inverness for a two week honeymoon on Thursday 16 July 1931.

(*H. C. Casserley*)

5. All the atmosphere of old Euston as the departure time approaches of a steam hauled top express is summed up in this scene on a winter's day in 1951. The heat and smell of the locomotive accompanied by the roar of safety valves, and the tartan-backed headboard, all added to the excitement of a long journey, in this case 401½ miles non-stop except for a change of crew near Carlisle. On this day the 'Royal Scot' is in the hands of de-streamlined Coronation pacific No. 46235 CITY OF BIRMINGHAM and its footplate crew. It is seen being admired at the wooden-planked end of Platform 13 as the time ticks on towards 10.00 a.m.   (*Nigel Dyckhoff*)

6 (opposite above). At Euston station on Saturday 9 July 1960 a passenger sits on his suitcase and contemplates the lines of Fowler Patriot 4-6-0 No. 45504 ROYAL SIGNALS as it emerges from the gloom within to commence its journey hauling the 4.25 p.m. train to Birmingham. 45504 was one of the stud of ex-LMS locomotives allocated to the ex-Midland shed at Bristol (Barrow Road) after its transfer to the Western Region in 1958, hence its 82E shed plate.   (*Nigel Mundy – RCTS Scotland*)

7 (opposite below). The unique B.R. Riddles class 8P Caprotti pacific No. 71000 DUKE OF GLOUCESTER had only just been built in 1954 and creates a lot of interest while standing in Euston at the head of the down 'Midday Scot'. This train became a regular turn for the 'Duke'.   (*Tony Heighton*)

8. A 'Freedom of Scotland' silver ticket providing seven days unlimited travel – one of the many different deals for railway travellers proposing to visit Scotland. (*Colin Stacey Collection*)

9. 'The Caledonian' was introduced in the summer of 1957 as a high-speed service each way between Euston and Glasgow Central and with one stop at Carlisle was scheduled to take 6 hours 40 minutes. With seventeen minutes to go to its 4.15 p.m. departure time from Euston, the safety valves are already lifting on Coronation pacific No. 46242 CITY OF GLASGOW while the passengers say their goodbyes on Friday 22 April 1960. (*The Transport Treasury*)

10. You would be hard pushed to locate a finer view of Camden bank than this, photographed from the bridge on Mornington Street, early morning on Saturday 25 July 1953, a view that was possible only with the use of a ladder. Central to the panorama is Stanier Jubilee No. 45721 IMPREGNABLE on a relief 'Irish Mail' (reporting No. 49B) forging its way up the bank with its rake of red and cream coaches ably assisted at the rear by the 0-6-0 tank that brought the stock into Euston station. Adjacent to the carriage sheds, rebuilt Patriot No. 45523 BANGOR stands with the stock of the timetabled 'Irish Mail' which is about to be backed down into Euston. On the left a Stanier 'Black 5' stands down the underpass. (R. J. Blenkinsop)

11.Viewed from the same location as illustration 10, this time on Saturday 22 August 1953, Coronation class pacific No. 46251 CITY OF NOTTINGHAM strides up Camden Bank at just gone 10.00 a.m. with the down 'Royal Scot'. In the carriage shed, Jinty 0-6-0 tank No. 47522 marshals stock in the form of a GWR Collett 9'-3" Brake Composite.

(R. J. Blenkinsop)

12 (above). The typically busy environment of a large locomotive shed is seen here at Chalk Farm's Camden depot late in 1936. The latest form of motive power is on view as the Coronation pacifics did not make their appearance until the following year. Receiving attention are Stanier Jubilee 4-6-0s Nos. 5711 COURAGEOUS, 5601 BRITISH GUIANA, 5689 AJAX, 5714 REVENGE and 5687 NEPTUNE accompanied by Princess Royal pacific Nos. 6209 PRINCESS BEATRICE and 6204 PRINCESS LOUISE. All are in the process of being serviced and cleaned prior to departing for Euston to pick up their rostered trains. *(Daily Herald)*

13 (right). It is March 1932 and the old Camden loco shed is being demolished, the new structure having been already erected and in use at the rear. Inside the old shed are class members from the previous LNWR regime in the shape of Bowen-Cooke Prince of Wales 4-6-0 No. 5686 ANGLIA followed by two of Bowen-Cooke's elegant Claughton 4-6-0s with another on the adjacent road. These two photographs show just how much the express motive power changed at Camden in the short time after William Stanier's arrival at the LMS in January 1932. *(Central Press)*

14. The view from E. R. Wethersett's bedroom window at 85 Harvest Road, London NW6 gave this glimpse of down trains as they passed the London & Provincial Steam Laundry's branch at Kilburn Park. On Saturday 1 September 1929 Fowler Royal Scot 4-6-0 No. 6105 CAMERON HIGHLANDER in original condition gets to grips with a northbound working.

(E. R. Wethersett – N.R.M)

15. Arriving home after a week working in London, one way of winding down was to photograph a few trains passing your window. Many such views were taken by Henry Casserley from the bedroom of 7 Castle Hill Close, Berkhamstead. This one around 6 p.m. on Friday 26 May 1936 shows Stanier 8F 2-8-0 No. 8106 working purposefully by with a northbound goods train on the down slow line. A selection of the once familiar private owner coal wagons stand in the adjacent sidings.

(H. C. Casserley)

16. It was an overcast day at Willesden on Saturday 29 October 1938 but fortunately that did not deter the photographer from capturing the powerful image of the down 'Midday Scot' due out from Euston at 2 p.m. and seen here well into its stride some 5½ miles into the journey. The train, previously known as 'The Corridor' is headed by one of Stanier's masterpieces, Coronation class pacific No. 6231 DUCHESS OF ATHOLL in original single chimney form, and then less than four months old.

(*E. R. Wethersett – Rail Archive Stephenson*)

17. While Kilsby tunnel was being built, the south section of the London & Birmingham Railway terminated at Denbigh Hall, just north of Bletchley. Temporary platforms were built and passengers transported between Denbigh and Rugby by coach and horses from April to September 1838 when the line was opened. On Tuesday 12 March 1959, Hughes Mogul 2-6-0 No. 42870 heads a northbound goods past Denbigh Hall signalbox and over an almost deserted Watling Street (A5).

(*Northampton Chronicle & Echo*)

18. The fireman on Stanier Jubilee 4-6-0 No. 45631 TANGANYIKA leaves the water scoop down too long and the front coach gets a good drenching as water cascades from the locomotive's tender. The train is an up relief from Manchester and is seen hurrying over Castlethorpe troughs on Saturday 7 May 1955.

(*D. M. C. Hepburne-Scott – Rail Archive Stephenson*)

19. The 'Great Cutting' at Roade opened in September 1838. It is 1½ miles long and in places the track is fifty feet below the surface which necessitated the removal of some one million cubic yards of material. The line to Northampton, excavated at a later date and opened in December 1881, caused major problems as the overlying rock slipped on the wet clay, requiring the surface levels on that side to be reduced and massive retaining walls to be constructed. These were further supported by steel stanchions held apart by overhead girders as shown in this view looking towards Black Bridge at the northern end of the cutting. Here in the late 1930s, Hughes/Fowler 'Crab' 2-6-0 No. 2817 eases up the gradient from Northampton with a Euston-bound local as workmen carry out maintenance on the adjacent retaining wall.

(Frank Raymond Williams – Peter Boswell Collection)

Panned photography takes skill to obtain sharp locomotive images and Michael Mensing succeeded very well, especially as he mainly resorted to panning when the weather was unsatisfactory for normal photography. Here around Rugby are interesting profile comparisons of Stanier locomotives at speed.

22. Jubilee No. 45584 NORTH WEST FRONTIER on the combined 12.00 noon Euston to Crewe and 12.27 p.m. Watford Junction to Birmingham New Street near Hillmorton approaching Rugby on the Northampton line. The train would be split during its stop at Rugby, Whit Monday 26 May 1958.

20 (opposite above). Coronation class No. 46237 CITY OF BRISTOL has just taken water from Newbold troughs on the Trent Valley line while heading the up 'Royal Scot' on Tuesday 29 April 1958. By the look of the tender, a good tonnage of coal has been used during the trip southwards.

21 (opposite below). 'Black 5' No. 45413 and rebuilt Royal Scot No. 46142 THE YORK AND LANCASTER REGIMENT double-head the up 'Red Rose' on the Trent Valley line, Whit Monday 26 May 1958.
(all three by Michael Mensing)

23 (opposite above). Late afternoon on a February day in 1939 the photographer waited on the bridge at Gayton Loops, just north of Blisworth station, hoping the light would hold out long enough to photograph the up 'Royal Scot', often hauled at this time by one of Stanier's streamlined pacifics. When it duly arrived the whole ensemble reflected the setting sun as the highly polished crimson and gold-striped Coronation pacific No. 6225 DUCHESS OF GLOUCESTER swept the train on towards its appointed 5.25 p.m. Euston arrival time. (*W. J. S. Meredith*)

24 (opposite below). Thursday 23 September 1937 finds an ex-LNWR 'Super D' class G1 0-8-0 No. 8908 wheezing along beside the Oxford Canal at Brinklow with a northbound cattle train. This locomotive was one of the class originally built as a Webb four-cylinder compound in May 1902, being converted to a class G1 simple in August 1923. The narrow boats are well laden with coal as they head south in the usual pairing of leading powered boat pulling the unpowered 'butty' boat. They will join up with the Grand Union Canal at Braunston on which they will head towards London. (*T. G. Hepburn – Rail Archive Stephenson*)

25 (below). During a relatively peaceful period at Crewe station near 6 a.m. on Sunday morning 1 June 1958, steam hisses from the cylinder drain cocks on Stanier Coronation pacific No. 46231 DUCHESS OF ATHOLL, drifting back around the locomotive and coaches. The well-groomed Polmadie Duchess had just drawn in with a northbound very long and heavy passenger, parcels and newspaper train. (*Dave Pick*)

26 (left). The non-streamlined version of the Stanier Coronation pacific stands in all its glory outside Crewe North shed on Sunday 14 August 1938 represented by the newly constructed No. 6234 DUCHESS OF ABERCORN. It was trials with this locomotive in first single and then double blastpipe forms during February 1939 that showed the vast improvement in power output with the double blastpipe and resulted in all the class being fitted likewise. Fortunately the double chimney did not spoil the locomotive's classic lines, being well positioned on the smokebox barrel. *(Les Hanson)*

27 (below). An interesting comparison of the old and new outside Crewe works on Sunday 14 August 1938. Ex-LNWR Webb 'Cauliflower' 0-6-0 No. 8588 built in March 1901 awaits attention alongside Stanier pacific No. 6225 DUCHESS OF GLOUCESTER, just three months old. The old lady may look antiquated against the 'Duchess', but still has a nicely balanced shape even without her tender. *(Les Hanson)*

28. You could not pass Crewe without a glimpse into its famous locomotive works and here in the erecting shop it was as busy and as noisy as ever on an August day in 1954. Prominent is newly built Riddles Britannia pacific No. 70053 nearing completion and soon to be transferred to the paint shop. In the background No. 70054 also takes shape. They would be named MORAY FIRTH and DORNOCH FIRTH respectively. *(Keith Locke)*

A RETURN TICKET TO SCOTLAND

29 (right). One of the many spur lines to cities and towns emanating from our route north provided access to the atmospheric environs around the cutting complex at Lime Street station, Liverpool, some distance from the West Coast main line but well worth a visit. Here on a January morning in 1949 'Royal Scot' 4-6-0 No. 46123 ROYAL IRISH FUSILIER suffers a wheel slip on the damp greasy rails at the station while endeavouring to get its train on the move for an attack on the 1 in 83 gradient up to Edge Hill, the resulting steam and smoke display proving quite spectacular. 46123 would undergo a metamorphosis during May of the same year, emerging from Crewe works with a Stanier taper boiler and the distinctive curved smoke deflectors completely transforming its looks as well as enhancing its performance. (*Wharton Collection*)

31. 10.32 a.m. on a summer Saturday in 1964 and the procession of holiday specials to Blackpool is already under way at Preston (North Union) station. Working purposefully through platform 5, Farnley Junction based Stanier Jubilee No. 45643 RODNEY makes its presence felt while laying a smokescreen under the overall roof with a special from Leeds. The travelling passengers are no doubt anxious to reach the sea, sand and bright lights of the resort as soon as possible.

(Roger Bailey)

30 (opposite below). The magnificent signal gantry to the north of Preston station fittingly frames Riddles Britannia No. 70013 OLIVER CROMWELL wreathed in steam as the locomotive heads one of the many specials arranged by railway societies as steam haulage drew to a close in August 1968. This one is heading north on Saturday 13 April 1968.

(John Hunt)

32 (above). An excellent overall view of Carnforth depot, but one that was only achievable by the photographer climbing a soot-encrusted sycamore tree and ending up with a liberal coating of grime for his effort. As usual this busy shed is packed with steam locomotives on Wednesday 22 June 1966, even though their demise was on the horizon, although Carnforth was to be one of the last three active steam depots, not closing until August 1968. To complete the scene a railwayman hitches a lift on Stanier 'Black 5' No. 45421 as it works past with a northbound goods train. (*Ben Ashworth*)

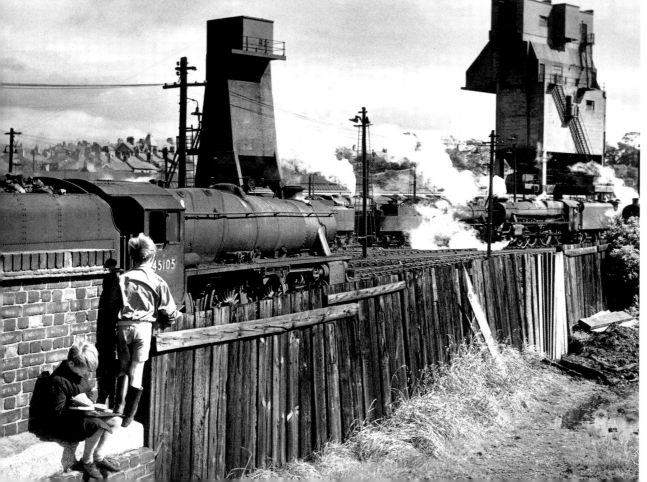

33 (left). "You shout them out and I'll write them down." This is a scene which will bring back childhood memories of days gone by for many readers at Carnforth on Monday 27 June 1966. Unfortunately Stanier 'Black 5' No. 45105 partly obstructs the lads' view as they enjoy a day in the field next to the shed. Surrounded by many locomotives, the huge mechanical coaling and ash plants dominate the yard.

(*Ben Ashworth*)

34. Framed by the canopy at Oxenholme on Saturday 18 June 1966, Stanier 8F 2-8-0 No. 48712 slogs its way through the station on a northbound goods approximately half way up the long steady 13 mile climb to Grayrigg summit. On this day a Fairburn 2-6-4 tank from Carnforth shed was providing banking assistance (Oxenholme shed having closed in June 1962) and the driver of the 8F would be hoping for a push up to the summit as he approaches the advance warning repeater disc signals under the canopy. The signals inform him that the unsighted starter signal around the curve at the north end of the platform is giving him a clear road, not that any advance warning is required in this instance with the goods train moving at walking pace.

(Ben Ashworth)

36. A panorama so typical of Westmorland fell country and its associated weather around Shap Fell as the sun breaks through a stormy sky to highlight the distant landscape around Greenholme on Thursday 28 December 1967. Down at rail level it's the usual all-out effort as Britannia 4-6-2 No. 70013 OLIVER CROMWELL toils up the gradient towards Scout Green with a northbound goods while Standard class 4 4-6-0 No. 75037 pushes from the rear.

(*John Hunt*)

35 (opposite). A thunderous exhaust from Riddles Britannia 4-6-2 No. 70027 RISING STAR darkens the sky as the locomotive's wheels fight for adhesion on the damp rails just north of Tebay station on Saturday 1 April 1967. The driver was endeavouring to get his early morning goods train on the move for an attack of the 1 in 75 Shap incline but appears to have been a little over zealous with the regulator. The locomotive shed, home of the Shap bankers, is silhouetted in the right background.

(*John Hunt*)

37. A truly impressive sight near Shap on Monday 24 July 1939 and one not to be repeated for too much longer as the Second World War put an end to the prestigious 'Coronation Scot' service and also the cleanliness of the Streamliners. Fortunately the photographer had the presence of mind to stand back from the lineside for a panoramic view as Stanier Coronation pacific No. 6222 QUEEN MARY powered past with the down train, the stripes that continued from the locomotive along the carriages highlighted as he stopped the action with a shutter speed of 1/800th of a second.

(*Maurice Earley N.R.M. MWE10/8*)

38. Fourteen coaches and no banker, so it's not surprising that Fowler Patriot 4-6-0 No. 45519 LADY GODIVA is hurling smoke to the heavens on a very cold Good Friday 8 April 1950 while hauling the 9.35 a.m. Crewe to Perth train near Salterwath on the climb to Shap summit. As the photographer wrote, "He thought the fireman even on so cold a day would have been a great deal warmer at Shap Wells than the loco's namesake would have been on a very hot blooded horse."

(*Derek Cross*)

39. A glorious autumnal day by the lineside in the beautiful Lune gorge with steam hauled trains passing by. What a civilised way to spend a few hours! In this setting, Stanier Jubilee No. 45717 DAUNTLESS sweeps over Dillicar troughs with a down Liverpool to Glasgow express in the mid 1950s. Dillicar was one of eleven sets of water troughs on the ex-LNWR and Caledonian lines between Euston and Glasgow Central, far more than on any other Anglo-Scottish route.

(*W. J. V. Anderson – Rail Archive Stephenson*)

40. At the north end of Carlisle Citadel station around 7.15 p.m. on an autumn evening in 1957, Stanier Coronation pacific No. 46240 CITY OF COVENTRY catches the low light standing at platform 3 with the down 'Midday Scot'. In the bay on the left is the front end of an ex-LNER J39 0-6-0. These locomotives from Carlisle Canal shed were regularly employed on the Silloth and Langholm trains.   (*The Transport Treasury*)

41. Carlisle Citadel station was a hive of activity for most of the time with train and locomotive movements aplenty. In this scene at the north end on Friday 9 July 1954, Gresley A3 pacific No. 60097 HUMORIST from Haymarket shed eases forward from the main line platform with an express bound for Edinburgh via the Waverley route. The movement is watched closely by one of the local 'spotting' fraternity, while on the adjacent line Carlisle Kingmoor based Stanier 'Black 5' No. 44675 awaits its next turn of duty.   (*John Harrison*)

42. Observations under the station roof at Carlisle Citadel on Thursday 14 May 1936 give just a flavour of the different railway companies whose lines converged on this important joint station like spokes in the hub of a wheel. One of ex-Midland's 7'-0" Deeley Compound 4-4-0s No. 1022 waits to take over a train heading south via the Settle route. In bay 1 an ex-North Eastern D17 4-4-0 No. 1924 stands with the 10.30 a.m. train from Newcastle, the leading two vehicles being standard LMS horseboxes, while the coach adjacent to the Compound is an ex-North British Corridor 3rd which had arrived over the Waverley route.

(H. C. Casserley)

43. At Carlisle Citadel station, the driver of Riddles Britannia pacific No. 70049 SOLWAY FIRTH eases the locomotive back in preparation to take over an Anglo-Scottish express for the final leg to Glasgow on Thursday 10 August 1967. When the photographer lifted his camera, there was no sign of the fireman, so it was pure good fortune he happened to climb back onto the footplate at just the right moment. (*Trevor Ermel*)

44. The wheel tapper keeps his eye on the job at Carlisle Citadel on Saturday 5 August 1967 as the Saturdays only train from Birmingham to Glasgow having travelled over the Settle and Carlisle line from Leeds arrives behind Stanier Jubilee No. 45562 ALBERTA. The immaculately turned-out Jubilee was the last of the class to be withdrawn in November the same year. The Stanier 'Black 5' No. 44802 is waiting to take over the Saturdays only Dundee to Blackpool train.
(Trevor Ermel)

CARRYING THE PASSENGERS

45. McIntosh/Pickersgill 0-4-4 tank No. 15238 was one of the class built with strengthened buffer beams and other slight modifications for banking purposes. At Beattock on Saturday 1 August 1931 it carries out the job for which it was designed, providing rear end assistance to the 3.00 p.m. Manchester to Edinburgh train hauled by an LMS Compound 4-4-0.

(*H. C. Casserley*)

46 (above). A rather dismal day at Beattock station befits the occasion of the last day of passenger services on the Moffat branch on Saturday 4 December 1954 and will also be the last day for the porter's customary shout "Beattock, change here for Moffat". In the main line platform Britannia pacific No. 70053 (not yet named MORAY FIRTH) waits for a banker to buffer up to the heavy morning train from Liverpool and Manchester to Glasgow Central for a push up to the summit. The connecting Moffat branch train coupled behind ex-Caley 0-4-4 tank No. 55232 will leave the bay platform at 1.55 p.m.   (W.A.C. Smith)

47 (right). A small group of railwaymen and passengers gather round 0-4-4 tank No. 55232 at Moffat station, terminus of the two mile branch on the last day of public passenger services, all no doubt saddened by the occasion. Due out at 3.05 p.m. the locomotive will propel its single coach train (which was authorised on the branch) back to Beattock on Saturday 4 December 1954. The branch was opened in 1883 and after closure to passengers continued in use for goods traffic until April 1964.   (W.A.C. Smith)

48. On the bright frosty morning of Monday 19 December 1960 Stanier pacific No. 46246 CITY OF MANCHESTER puts up a superb exhaust as steam condenses in the cold air while making the southbound ascent to Beattock Summit with the up 'Royal Scot'. The smoke deflectors designed to lift the exhaust clear of the cab to aid the driver's vision work admirably as steam swirls around the base of the chimney. (*W. J. V. Anderson – Rail Archive Stephenson*)

49. In contrast to the previous picture, this time on the northbound climb to Beattock Summit, the exhaust from Riddles Clan pacific No. 72009 CLAN STEWART blackens the sky as the fireman piles coal into the firebox. The Clan is making an unassisted climb at Harthope as it pounds by with the 9.25 a.m. Crewe to Perth and Aberdeen on Tuesday 11 August 1964.

(*J. S. Whiteley*)

50. On the day of H.M. Queen Elizabeth II's Coronation on Tuesday 2 June 1953, Polmadie shed had put the cleaners to work on their Stanier pacific No. 46220 CORONATION and sent it out in pristine condition complete with a crown headboard to work the up 'Royal Scot'. After the train's 10.00 a.m. departure from Glasgow Central we see the ensemble getting into its stride as it passes through Eglinton Street station at the beginning of the long trip south.

(K. K. *MacKay*)

51. The Queen Mother travelled down from Ballater to open the Scottish Industrial Exhibition at Kelvin Hall in Glasgow on Thursday 2 September 1954. The return journey left Buchanan Street at 5.30 p.m. and is seen passing St Rollox station behind highly polished Stanier 'Black 5' No. 45499. Adjacent to the Royal Train, the 1.15 p.m. from Aberdeen has been held so as not to pass the Royal Train in the tunnel. (*W.A.C. Smith*)

52. Some of the local populace have obviously found out that the Royal Train would be spending the night on the Moffat branch on Monday 7 July 1958 and have turned out to see if they can get a glimpse of its occupants. Having arrived at Beattock from the north of Scotland, the ten coach train has been reversed and curves away from the main line towards Moffat behind Stanier 'Black 5' No. 44902. (*David Anderson*)

53. The original four track bridge over the Clyde in Glasgow was constructed for the passage of trains into what was then the new Central station opened in 1879 and is seen here with a train from the south entering the station in 1960. The station and bridge were soon found to be of inadequate size for the amount of traffic, resulting in the building of a greatly enlarged Central station and a new nine track bridge adjacent to the old one, all of which was completed in 1906. In 1908 electro-pneumatic signalling was installed, worked from a power signalbox situated between the two bridges, part of which can be seen upper left. The signals, some of which can be seen overhead, had a Banner-type indicator informing the train crew which platform the train was signalled into, in this case platform 1. The small signal below the main signal indicated whether the platform was clear up to the buffer stops. At the entrance to the station, one of the 0-4-4 tanks is on pilot duty. When the station area was re-signalled in 1961, this bridge was removed. *(P. Hay)*

55 (opposite below). The maze of points and signals on the bridge over the River Clyde and beyond at Glasgow Central is shown to good advantage in this view from the platform end on Tuesday, 29 July 1958. On the left Fairburn 2-6-4 No. 42275 leaves with a local train. The banner below the signal indicates to the driver that he will be taking line 2 towards his destination. *(Tony Heighton)*

54 (left). The British Railways Standard 2-6-4 tanks were delivered to Scotland soon after they were introduced, No. 80027 being in the first batch arriving at Polmadie on 4 January 1952. Still in pristine condition on Monday 14 July 1952, the locomotive catches the low sun while crossing the Clyde Bridge running into Glasgow Central at 9.11 p.m. with the 8.05 p.m. local from Gourock.

(*Ron Gammage*)

56 (above). On the morning of Tuesday, 29 July 1958, Riddles Standard class 5 4-6-0 No. 73055 works its way out of Glasgow Central station. The route indicator on the centre lamp bracket is set for an ordinary service train to the Cathcart Outer Circle line. (*Tony Heighton*)

57 (below). Looking out over the Clyde bridges at 10.00 p.m. on Saturday 14 April 1948, ex-Caledonian 0-4-4 tank No. 15224 makes its way into Glasgow Central station with a Cathcart Inner Circle train. (*H. C. Casserley*)

58. 10.00 a.m. departure time is approaching at Glasgow Central and Polmadie's Coronation pacific No. 46232 DUCHESS OF MONTROSE has been fully prepared at the head of the up 'Royal Scot' complete with the tartan-backed headboard on Tuesday 23 May 1961. In LMS days the 'Royal Scot' carriage sets were turned daily, a pilot engine attaching itself to the rear after the train's arrival, and with the train engine pushing the train would proceed up the Coast Line to Shields No. 1 Junction where it would reverse to follow the Pollock & Govan Railway section to Gushetfaulds Junction. *(Ray Reed)*

59. A photograph oozing with atmosphere at platform 3 inside Glasgow Central as the signal drops above parallel boiler Royal Scot No. 6102 BLACK WATCH giving the all clear to get a relief 'Royal Scot' away towards London on Saturday 5 October 1946. The locomotive was rebuilt with a Stanier taper boiler in October 1949. For any young trainspotter south of Crewe 'Black Watch' was one of the locomotives on their most wanted list as it seemed very reluctant to travel far into English territory.

(H. C. Casserley)

60 (opposite above). Drummond Jumbo 0-6-0 No. 17447 was one of the class members fitted with steam heating pipes and vacuum brakes, making it ideal for drawing in and taking out coaching stock at Glasgow Central station. With a smoke haze lingering under the roof on Saturday 5 October 1946, the locomotive stands with the stock of the mail train adjacent to platform 11. On the platform a lorry is piled high with mailbags.   (H. C. Casserley)

61 (opposite below). Smoke and steam swirling around under the roof at Glasgow Central highlights the shafts of sunlight penetrating through on Monday 12 September 1955. Down below, one of the station pilots, ex-Caley 0-4-4 tank No. 55237 is about to detach a Royal Mail van from a 'Parly' (Carlisle local) after arrival at platform 4, while, over in platform 7, BR Standard 2-6-4 tank No. 80056 waits to depart with a Cathcart Circle train.

(H. C. Casserley)

62. Friday night 15 October 1920 in Glasgow Central, and Caledonian Railway Pickersgill class 3P 4-4-0 No. 78, built at St Rollox works only six weeks previously, gleams under the station lights, waiting at the head of the 10.20 p.m. sleeping car express for London Euston. These locomotives were the last development of McIntosh's Dunalastairs although they were not considered to be as good as the superheated Dunalastair IV. The first vehicle is a WCJS 57-foot Brake composite followed by an LNWR/WCJS parcels sorting van. *(L.C.G.B. – Ken Nunn Collection)*

63 (opposite above). Thanks to James Ness, the innovative and energetic General Manager of the Scottish Region in the 1950s, Caledonian Railway 4-2-2 No. 123, built by Neilson & Co in 1886 and preserved at the St Rollox Works since 1935, was restored to working order early in 1958, being joined the following year by GNSR No. 49, H.R. No. 103 and N.B.R. No. 256 to form a quartet of historic locomotives available for both public excursions and private charter until a change of management saw them retired to the Glasgow Museum of Transport in 1966. No. 123's first public outing, accompanied by a pair of restored Caledonian coaches, was in April 1958 from Glasgow (Buchanan Street) to Perth. On Saturday 17 May 1958 it ran from St Enoch to Ayr at a fare of 5/- return and was photographed at platform 2 prior to its 1.55 p.m. departure as another Caley veteran, 0-4-4 tank No. 55225, built at St Rollox in 1914, drew into platform 3 with empty stock. No. 123 had been given a fast timing of 52 minutes for the 40¾ miles (via Troon) which, in the event, it was not quite able to obtain. St Enoch station had been opened in 1876 and was closed in 1966. *(W.A.C. Smith)*

64 (below). A two week programme of "Excursions by Historic Locomotives" for the Scottish Industries Exhibition at Glasgow commenced on Thursday 5 September 1959 for which the quartet of preserved Scottish locomotives was joined by former GWR 4-4-0 No. 3440 CITY OF TRURO. No. 3440's inaugural run was, in fact, on 3 September with a six coach train from Montrose, GNSR No. 49 GORDON HIGHLANDER being provided as pilot, and was photographed upon arrival at platform 11 of Glasgow Central station. This view gives a good impression of the station's magnificent roof, recently refurbished by Railtrack at a cost of £1m.

(W. A. C. Smith)

65. Henry Casserley and his son Richard were fascinated by Glasgow Central Low Level station where steam locomotives still hauled the trains through soot-encrusted tunnels and even in the 1950s was like stepping back in time to the Victorian era, the system having being constructed in the 1890s. Attempting to capture on film the atmosphere that existed in these gloomy confines where time exposures were essential was a real challenge, attempted by very few people. Fortunately Henry succeeded very well, as the next four images show. On Monday 21 April 1952 Fairburn 2-6-4 tank No. 42699 is viewed from the island platform as it prepares to depart on a morning train to the west.

(H. C. Casserley)

66. Glasgow Central Low Level was the only station on the line with an island platform having up and down running tracks on one side and up and down passing loops on the other side. These passing loops were controlled by signalboxes at either end of the station, one of which can be seen on the right of the photograph. On Monday 12 September 1955, passengers await the arrival of a westbound train, while Stanier 2-6-2 tank No. 40188 prepares to leave from the island platform with the 1.55 p.m. train from Possil to Carmyle. (H. C. Casserley)

67. Glasgow Central Low Level was an eerie place with echoing passageways and an almost unnatural quietness broken every few minutes by the rumble of trams passing along the city's busy streets a few feet overhead. With the trains' arrival from the fume-filled tunnel, smoke and steam would swirl around under the large flat roof area, its only means of escape at the side of the station. All of this created a rather poor environment for its everyday travelling passengers. On Monday 21 April 1952, Stanier 2-6-2 Tank No. 40177 creates the scene while awaiting departure with the 8.15 a.m. train from Whifflet to Maryhill.

(*H. C. Casserley*)

68. One description of what it was like to travel behind steam from Glasgow Central Low Level was written by C. Hamilton Ellis in the January 1938 *Railway Magazine*, "Sombre sulphurous and Plutonian the line may be but to a good railwayist it is a most fascinating place. The locomotives on it do not condense, a fact which increases the Miltonesque effect of their exits and entrances. There is something very stimulating, even in the sensation of climbing into one of a long row of lit compartments in the midst of a dim haze and moving off with the steamy windows tightly shut, into a darkness even more profound to the accompaniment of a deep thudding exhaust."

On Saturday 10 September 1955 Stanier 2–6–2 tank No. 40187 stands in the station with the 12.00 noon Rutherglen to Balloch train. The buildings on the island platform can be seen to the left of the locomotive.   (*H. C. Casserley*)

69. On 22 July 1959, Standard class 4MT 2-6-0 No. 76002 runs into Anderston Cross station with the 5.40 p.m. from Maryhill (Central) to Whifflet (Upper). The Glasgow Central Low Level line opened in 1896, passed beneath city streets jammed with horse-drawn traffic, and intrigued the press with "tastefully designed stations" and "lady booking clerks". The station was unusual in that it had a single island platform with a running line either side. The line was steam worked although the Caley had obtained Parliamentary approval for electrification of its tramway network in 1901. This, with its convenience, cleanliness and cheapness, brought an on-going decline to the line with passenger bookings at Anderston Cross dropping from 239,000 in 1913 to 76,706 in 1922 and 7,651 in 1949, and the station was closed, along with its neighbouring Stobcross, on 3 August 1959. Ironically, when the remainder of the system closed on 5 October 1964, it had outlived the trams by two years and Glasgow Corporation Transport Department was among objectors to its closure! Fifteen years later, part of the system was electrified and re-opened.

(*W. A. C. Smith*)

70. Glasgow Cross was another station on the Central Low Level line considered to be entirely underground, but it did have a small section open to the air for smoke ventilation. The driver of ex-Caley 'Jumbo' 0-6-0 No. 57444 has positioned his locomotive to make maximum use of this facility while standing with the 8.38 a.m. train from Possil to Rutherglen as the passengers head for the street above on Monday 8 July 1957.

71. (Inset) A view in the opposite direction along the platform into the gloom of the station interior.   (both *H. C. Casserley*)

72. On the sunny afternoon of Tuesday 6 August 1957 Motherwell depot's well turned out Stanier 'Black 5' No. 45433 makes an impressive sight blasting out of Glasgow Central with the 2.45 p.m. train to Hamilton Central which was extended through to Motherwell. The train destinations covered by the Caledonian route indicator (Hamilton, Strathaven and Lesmahagow) were worked almost exclusively at this time by 2-6-4 tanks, so the appearance of a 'Black 5' was most unusual. The only person on view at this busy station is the footplateman from the ex-Caley 0-4-4 tank working on station pilot duties.

(*A. G. Forsyth – Initial Photographs*)

73. On the very dull and cold evening of Friday 14 April 1958, Stanier 2-6-2 tank No. 40188 arrives at Clydebank Riverside station with the 4.26 p.m. from Balloch to Rutherglen. Waiting to board the train are workers from John Brown's shipyard whose buildings can be seen in the background. This was the birthplace of famous ships such as the *Queen Mary*, *Queen Elizabeth*, and the *Royal Yacht*, amongst many others, but by the 1970s (and under new ownership) it was fabricating oil rigs, and now it is closed. To the left of the signals are the station's terminal platforms.

(*W. A. C. Smith*)

74. With Rangers F.C. playing at home, Ibrox could be the venue for half-a-dozen or more football specials. On 17 May 1961, trains from Motherwell and Gourock respectively have arrived at the main platforms on the Paisley Joint line, the nearest one hauled by Fairburn 2-6-4 tank No. 42276, while fans from Glasgow (Central) are routed onto the old Govan branch, Somewhat surprisingly, Ibrox station was closed upon electrification of the line in 1967. (*W. A. C. Smith*)

75. This incredible lighting effect of sunlight and shadow obviously caught the photographer's eye at Glasgow St Enoch station round about lunchtime on Saturday 24 April 1948 and fortunately he could not resist taking the shot. The safety valves on Stanier 'Black 5' No. 4899 are just building up to a crescendo as the maximum boiler pressure of 225 p.s.i. is reached while awaiting the train's departure time from platform 1.

(*H. C. Casserley*)

76. Under the massive roof at Glasgow St Enoch station there is all the atmosphere of a large station at night as Glasgow & South Western Manson 4-4-0 No. 430 awaits departure with the 9.30 p.m. train to Kilmarnock on Monday 13 September 1920. By this time the locomotive had been rebuilt with a larger boiler and different cab under the auspices of Whitelegg (Locomotive Superintendent). The train is made up of a typical set of six-wheeled carriages. *(L.C.G.B. – Ken Nunn Collection)*

77. The Stanier Coronation pacifics were not a common sight at St Enoch, although they were seen there more frequently during the 1960s. On the very dull day of Tuesday 4 June 1963, No. 46249 CITY OF SHEFFIELD gives the appearance of imminent departure but there are still over twenty minutes to go before it will leave with the 5.30 p.m. semi fast to Carlisle. At the adjacent platform BR Standard class 4 2-6-0 No. 76114 is about to depart with the 5.07 p.m. train to Paisley. The buildings on the platforms contain parcel hoists for movement to and from the lower level. (*H. C. Casserley*)

78. Situated on the south side of Glasgow St Enoch, platform 9 was used mainly by trains heading for Scotland's south-west coastal area, and during the LMS era the 3 cylinder Compound 4-4-0s were familiar sights at this platform, working trains as far as Stranraer via Girvan. At this location on Friday 4 October 1946, LMS Compound No. 1183 has a full head of steam and the blower on while waiting to depart with the 1.34 p.m. train to Largs. On leaving the station's curved platforms, further tight curves had to be negotiated before reaching the bridge over the Clyde, making the squealing of wheel flanges on rails a familiar sound from both outgoing and incoming trains at the terminus. (*H. C. Casserley*)

79. What a pleasure it was for the photographer to find this ex-Glasgow & South Western locomotive in the old G & SW terminus of St Enoch simmering at the head of a mid-afternoon local train on Monday 11 August 1930. One of James Manson's most handsome class 495 4-6-0s No. 14670 built in 1910 was looking quite resplendent in work-worn but well burnished LMS livery that suited it well. During the pre grouping era the original livery would have been middle-green with black-and-white lining.

(*H. C. Casserley*)

80. The magnificent roof at Glasgow St Enoch station dwarfs everything beneath it in this view on Monday 6 August 1956. 204 feet wide and 83 feet high, it was certainly an impressive structure. In the shadow LMS 2P 4-4-0s Nos. 40644 and 40599 await departure from platforms 2 and 4 on local passenger services. At platform 3, B.R. Clan pacific No. 72007 CLAN MACKINTOSH is about to depart with a semi fast to Carlisle, while over at platform 1 Pickersgill 4-4-0 No. 54506 stands at the head of a train to Greenock (Princes Pier). It is hard to believe that in 1977 they just knocked it all down and St Enoch was no more.

(*W. S. Sellar*)

The 'Starlight Specials' were introduced in 1953 as a cheap form of overnight travel either way between the cities of Glasgow, Edinburgh and London. These trains ran through the summer months primarily for holidaymakers who would leave London or Scotland on a Friday night with a choice of returning in a 'Starlight Special' eight or fifteen days later. Advance booking was essential and the number of trains to run in either direction depended on loadings. During the early part of the season, trains were often combined and routed from Glasgow St Enoch via Edinburgh Waverley and Newcastle, arriving in London via the Great Central route into Marylebone, and vice versa. The service ceased at the end of 1962.

81 (above). On the wet miserable evening of Friday 11 May 1956, Haymarket depot's A3 pacific No. 60100 SPEARMINT stands at St Enochs platform 2 with the up 'Starlight Special' due out at 8.00 p.m. The train of red and cream coaches, the first two of which are an LMS 57-foot 'porthole' brake 3rd and an LMS 60-foot composite will travel via Edinburgh Waverley to London.   (*W. A. C. Smith*)

82 (right). On Friday 29 May 1959, double chimney A3 pacific No. 60057 ORMONDE has its fire stoked up in preparation for the 8.00 p.m. departure of the 'Starlight Special' for London again via the Edinburgh Waverley route.   (*W. A. C. Smith*)

83. The classic Midland and Glasgow & South Western express stands alongside platform 1 at Glasgow St Enoch on Wednesday 23 August 1961. The headboard looks rather weather-beaten and the Royal Scot none too clean, but the name "Thames-Clyde Express" immediately gives an air of importance to the train. Introduced in 1927, the up train left St Enoch at varying times over the years between 9.00 and 9.30 a.m., and during this era was often worked by a Leeds Holbeck-based Royal Scot, so it was rather unusual to find Kentish Town's No. 46132 THE KING'S REGIMENT LIVERPOOL in charge. Glasgow to London St Pancras via the Midland route was around 25 miles further with a more torturous gradient than the more direct line from Glasgow Central to Euston and could not compete timewise, but the scenery was glorious through the Pennines on the Settle & Carlisle.   (Ray Reed)

84. The other St Enoch station, photo-graphed on the afternoon of Friday 4 October 1946. This building, by architect James Miller, who was also responsible for several stations on the Central Low Level line, was the headquarters of the Glasgow District Subway Company which, ten days before the Christmas of 1896, opened a 6½ mile cable-operated circular railway beneath the streets of Glasgow. The system was acquired by Glasgow Corporation in 1923 and electrified in 1935, being thereafter officially known as 'the Underground', although, even in the present, it remains 'the Subway' to Glaswegians, despite a £60m mod-ernisation which took place in the early 1980s. The building is now a travel centre, access to the platforms being provided by escalators off to the right.

(H. C. Casserley)

85. At Partick Cross on the Glasgow Subway, an Inner Circle train arrives on Monday 11 August 1930, at the time when the 4'-0" gauge railway was cable-operated. The cars were provided with doors on one side only and had to be lifted through an access point in the roof to a higher level in order to carry out maintenance.

(H. C. Casserley)

86. Photographs of ex-Glasgow & South Western Railway locomotives after 1923 are not so numerous as those from other Scottish railway companies simply because they suffered most in the clearout after the grouping when the LMS was formed. Here at Glasgow St Enoch station on Thursday 30 July 1931, Manson 18 class (LMS 2P) 4-4-0 No. 14377 has its fire built up during a quiet spell while on station pilot duties. Thirteen of this class were built between 1907 and 1912 and all were withdrawn by the end of 1932.

(H. C. Casserley)

87. Here we see an impressive line-up of ex-Glasgow & South Western motive power at St Enoch, as one of Whitelegg's massive Baltic class 5P 4-6-4 tanks No. 15405 backs out of the station and is about to pass another of the class on Friday 11 April 1930. Introduced in 1922, a year before the grouping, only six were built, all carrying the unusual livery described as light olive green for the tanks, cab and bunker lined out with black and white, a red footplate and edging, and boiler cladding of unpainted blue steel. They must have looked quite spectacular. Between the two tanks stands a Smellie 4-4-0 of 1885 vintage No. 14135. There were various differences to locomotives of this class; this was one of two with small domed boilers that also retained a Stirling-type of half cab. All the locomotives in this view are painted in LMS livery.

(H. C. Casserley)

88. The Glasgow & South Western Railway in its heyday is seen here *c*.1900 as Manson 336 class 'Greenock Bogie' 4-4-0 No. 355 puts up a grand smoke display while attacking the climb from Greenock with an express bound for Glasgow St Enoch. When Whitelegg became the railway's locomotive superintendent in 1918 he instigated what was supposed to have been a number of improvements to the existing rundown locomotive stock, but according to reports by David L. Smith and other experts of the Glasgow & South Western he only succeeded in reducing their efficiency. No. 355 was later rebuilt with a large boiler and became LMS No. 14208.

(PC 1311 – Rail Archive Stephenson)

89. The Cathcart Circle was (and is) an institution in the life of the city's south side and had a novel written about it, dealt with thousands of football fans on occasions of major matches at Hampton Park and even fielded its own amateur football team in the 1930s. Ex-C.R. 0-4-4 tanks were used for many years and here No. 55201 is seen at Queens Park on Wednesday 16 May 1956 with the 4.30 p.m. Outer Circle train from Glasgow (Central).

(*W.A.C. Smith*)

90 (opposite above). Viewed from the platform of Kelvin Hall station on Thursday 6 June 1963, B.R. Standard 2-6-0 No. 76101 arrives with the 5.15 p.m. train from Dalmarnock to Old Kilpatrick, having just escaped the confines of Stobcross tunnel. Flanked by the flour mills on one side and the River Kelvin on the other, the station was originally named Partick Central.

(*H. C. Casserley*)

91 (left). The design of the station building at Mount Florida was typical of those on Glasgow's Cathcart Circle lines, built on an island platform and fitted with a wide glazed canopy all round. On Friday 5 July 1957 B.R. Standard 2-6-4 tank No. 80026 arrives with the 12.30 p.m. outer circle train from Glasgow Central (even though the C.R. route indicator is set for 'inner circle'). Mount Florida is the closest station to Hampden Park stadium and where numbers of football specials converged when internationals were being played.

(H. C. Casserley)

92 (left). A scene at Glasgow Buchanan Street station prior to the First World War finds Caledonian Connor 2-4-0 No. 474 approaching the platform end with a typical Caledonian 3 car set of six-wheelers (Brake Composite, all 3rd, Brake Composite) with a bogie strengthener bringing up the rear. The tall signal above the rear of the train would have required some substantial retaining wires to keep it stable especially in windy conditions.

(LGRP Richard Casserley Collection)

94. At Buchanan Street station on Saturday 7 October 1961 Stanier 'Black 5' No. 45474 simmers at the platform end after arrival with the 7.10 a.m. 'Bon Accord' express from Aberdeen, one of the prestigious 3-hour trains that was introduced in 1937 (only the 'up' train included the restaurant car and was so named on Saturdays). On the platform a lady sells refreshments from a trolley, presumably for those departing by train rather than those arriving. The name 'Bon Accord' was give to this train in 1949 when the name was reintroduced after the Second World War. Previously it was given to a differently timed train between the two cities. *(H. C. Casserley)*

93 (opposite below). Commuters head for their places of employment from within Glasgow's least attractive terminus of Buchanan Street at 8.10 a.m. on Tuesday 4 May 1965, 18 months before total closure (the Sunday services had already been diverted to Queen Street station). From this uninspiring station, the Caledonian's other terminus in the city, people departed for such destinations as Callander, Oban, Inverness, Dundee and Aberdeen, and it was here from 1962 that the Gresley A4s strutted their stuff on the famous three-hour expresses to the Granite City. *(H. C. Casserley)*

95. At platform 2 of Buchanan Street station, Gresley A4 pacific No. 60026 MILES BEEVOR is ready for its 153 mile dash to Aberdeen with the three-hour "Saint Mungo" express as the hands of the station clock approach departure time of 5.30 p.m. During the early 1960s there was a strong LNER atmosphere at Buchanan Street and on this occasion class B1 4-6-0 No. 61244 STRANG STEEL heads the 5.30 p.m. to Dunblane on Tuesday 31 August 1965.

(*W.A.C. Smith*)

96. At Glasgow's Buchanan Street station on the grey, damp evening of Saturday 25 April 1964, a few hardy souls gather at the platform end to witness Gresley A4 pacific No. 60026 MILES BEEVOR make a volatile departure out of platform 2 with the 5.30 p.m. 'Saint Mungo' express for Aberdeen. Caprotti Standard 5 No. 73152 waits, wreathed in steam, to follow with the 5.35 p.m. train to Dunblane.
(*W.A.C. Smith*)

97 (above). The final development of the 4-6-0 on the Highland Railway was Christopher Cumming Clan class 4P, eight of which were built between 1919 and 1921, primarily for use on trains between Inverness and Perth. With the introduction of the Stanier 'Black 5s', the Clans were transferred onto the route between Glasgow and Oban where they did sterling work. Here No. 14768 CLAN MACKENZIE blasts its way out of Glasgow Buchanan Street with the 9.45 a.m. train to Oban on Tuesday 21 June 1938. When built it carried the Highland Railway green livery. After the grouping this was changed to LMS red but by the time of this photograph it was LMS black with red lining. (H. C. Casserley)

98 (opposite above). On Monday 20 September 1910, immaculate McIntosh 'Dunalastair I' class 4-4-0 No. 721 DUNALASTAIR rolls in towards Princes Street station, Edinburgh, with the 8.50 a.m. train from Glasgow Central made up of a typical set of the company's 3rd class carriages, and passes a WCJS 42-foot composite coach. The locomotive, built in 1896, was the first in the series of the famous 'Dunalastair' 4-4-0s, named after the then Caledonian Company vice-chairman's estate near Pitlochry. (LCGB – Ken Nunn Collection)

99 (opposite below). Monday 20 September 1910 finds McIntosh 'Dunalastair II' 4-4-0 No. 766 DUNALASTAIR 2ND in pristine condition drawing out under the impressive Caledonian signal gantry at Edinburgh Princes Street with the 10.55 a.m. express to Glasgow Central. Built in 1897, this locomotive was the first of the 2nd series of Dunalastairs and remained in this form until 1914 when it was rebuilt with a superheated boiler. The unusual combination of Caledonian coaches consist of 6-wheel brake and six-wheel third followed by a set of the 65-foot long twelve-wheel non-corridor stock introduced by the Caledonian in 1906 for the Edinburgh – Glasgow service. Behind the signal gantry is the ornate glazed screen spanning the station's seven platforms. (LCGB – Ken Nunn Collection)

100. Edinburgh's Princes Street station was never overly busy but, just prior to its closure in September 1965, you could find more cars than passengers under the magnificent roof of this ex-Caledonian terminus in the capital. On this day a Stanier 'Black 5' has the station to itself, the exhaust beats echoing around as it backs out from the gracefully curved platforms. A both evocative and sad picture, as Princes Street and steam traction's usefulness were both coming to an irrevocable end. (*Malcolm Dunnett*)

101. On Thursday 29 April 1965 Edinburgh Princes Street station is alive with the sound of steam roaring into the roof void from the safety valves of Stanier 'Black 5' No. 45360, while, on platform 2, parcels and passengers are on the move. The train make-up is 61-foot Gresley Corridor Full Brake, GWR Collett Full Brake, and an LMS period 3 Stanier 'three set', forming the 6.50 p.m. train to Carstairs. A scene that hardly suggests closure is less than five months later. (*H. C. Casserley*)

102. This view inside Edinburgh Princes Street station on Saturday 20 June 1964 shows well the single span glazed roof structure and spacious circulating area including the large impressive clock that was supported on an ornate masonry structure, surrounded by the station's complex of facilities that includes Enquiry Office, Waiting and Refreshment Rooms, Lost Property Office and Bookstall, the Ticket Office being located in the centre of the circulating area. From the circulating area, passengers could gain access to the west end of Princes Street at the side of the Hotel entrance and down some steps to Lothian Road. The people chatting on platform 3 would soon have to board the all-stations stopping train to Carstairs as the 11.30 a.m. departure time approaches, hauled on this day by Fairburn 2-6-4 tank No. 42058 from Polmadie depot.   (*W. S. Sellar*)

103. This most unusual and rare view of the railway layout at Edinburgh Princes Street station was obtained from the roof by the photographer on Saturday 9 April 1960. All the tracks from the station and carriage sidings converge through the narrow opening between the tenement buildings, while all the lines on the left from Lothian Road goods depot converge into a short tunnel. On the tracks near to the signalbox a BR Standard 2-6-4 tank stands adjacent to the water column on the approach road to the turntable beyond, a Fairburn 2-6-4 tank heads under the signal gantry towards the station while an ex-Caledonian 0-6-0 shunts the station carriage sidings. After closure in September 1965, the Caledonian's terminus in the City along with its maze of tracks would gradually be erased from the landscape and, apart from the hotel, no trace remains.

(*W. S. Sellar*)

104. Smoke and steam in abundance plus a good layer of snow created this lively scene at Edinburgh Princes Street station as brand new British Railways Clan pacific No. 72002 makes a storming departure on Saturday 27 January 1952. Having yet to attend its official naming ceremony the CLAN CAMPBELL nameplates are temporarily covered over.

(*J. Robertson – Transport Treasury*)

105. Glimpsed between the buildings at Coalburn, Fairburn 2-6-4 tank No. 42243 arrives at the station with the 5.11 p.m. train from Glasgow on Thursday 4 July 1957. Construction of a Caledonian mineral line between Coalburn and Muirkirk commenced in the 1890s, but the line was never completed as apparently the G & SW could then have claimed running powers over the route. As there was no loop at Coalburn station, the empty stock of trains terminating there continued for ¾ mile to what was described as a "passenger" loop at Bankend Colliery for running round (additionally one or more sets of coaches were stabled there overnight). The line which was quite steeply graded continued for another three miles or so to Galawhistle, but this section appears to have become disused in LMS days. It included a viaduct which was demolished during the Second World War as a commando training exercise. Bankend Colliery was closed in 1958 and the loop became redundant when DMUs took over the Coalburn service. (H. C. Casserley)

106 (opposite above). An excellent panorama of the south platforms at Inverness prior to the First World War shows the unusual layout at this terminus station. Here most through trains from the south ran past the station on the Rose Street curve to clear the junction and then backed into the north platforms, likewise some trains from the north took the Rose Street curve and backed into the south platforms from the Welsh's Bridge Junction direction. At platform 1 Small Ben 4-4-0 No. 47 BEN A'BHUIRD stands with a train that has arrived from the north and reversed in, and behind the train stands a Highland mail van. At platform 2 a Loch class 4-4-0 piloting a Castle class 4-6-0 are given a clear road for the train's departure while Jones 2-4-0 tank No. 58 BURGHEAD is on station pilot duties at platform 4. In the loading dock between platforms 1 and 2, a motor car has been loaded onto a wagon, at this time quite a rare sight. (Richard Casserley Collection)

107 (left). Carlisle Kingmoor-based 'Crab' 2-6-0 No. 42884 was about to travel even further afield at Paisley Gilmour Street on a not untypical wet summer Saturday, 4 August 1962. Although looking exceedingly grimy, the Mogul is certainly not short of steam as it prepares to depart with the 8.58.a.m. train to Aberdeen. The canopies to the station are supported by lattice girders thus avoiding the need for obstructive columns on the platform.

(R. A. F. Puryer)

108. The weather is not co-operating again as a so-called 'Summer Saturday' excursion romps through Irvine station behind Stanier 'Black 5' No. 45486, whose train is composed entirely of Scottish Eastern Region stock on 4 August 1962. Having worked out from Ayr, the ensemble heads north on the Glasgow & South Western line as a GPO van driver trudges back to his vehicle after collecting the mail.

(R. A. F. Puryer)

109 (opposite above). It really wasn't a day to be hanging around stations at Gourock on Friday 6 October 1961 where it was wet and miserable and daylight struggled to penetrate the thick grey clouds. At the platform, BR Standard class 5 4-6-0 No. 73099 stands wreathed in steam and the blower on, awaiting departure time with the 10.35 a.m. train to Glasgow Central.

(H. C. Casserley)

110 (below). More rain, this time at Motherwell on the afternoon of Friday 3 August 1962 and the majority of the people on the platform quite sensibly shelter under the canopy as Stanier Princess Royal pacific No. 46201 PRINCESS ELIZABETH slackens off for the curve through the station with an express from Euston bound for Perth and Aberdeen. Typical of the area, the station is bare, smoke-stained and functional, with no trace of flowers or greenery whatsoever. (R. A. F. Puryer)

111 (above). McIntosh 812 class 0-6-0 No. 57559 at Leith (North) terminus with the 12.05 p.m. to Edinburgh (Princes Street) on 21 May 1955. The fare of fourpence return of the 5½ mile journey, taking 20 minutes and with six stops, was remarkable value even by 1950's standards but closure came in 1962 after dieselisation. A tram on service 23 passes along Lindsay Road from Granton, but Edinburgh ended this enlightened form of city transport the following year. (W.A.C. Smith)

113. Stranraer Harbour station seen from an excellent viewpoint on Friday 14 June 1963 shows to good effect the overall layout with an array of goods ready for transporting to their respective destinations or loading into the "Caledonian Princess" for the voyage to Larne in Northern Ireland. Four roads at the station are taken up with stock while Stanier 'Black 5' No. 44723 stands with the 1.40 p.m. train to Dumfries. If the signalman suffered from vertigo he would not fancy going round the back of his signalbox for it is a very long drop into Loch Ryan. Trains arriving at the station would have their coaches propelled back to the junction after unloading and then pulled around into Stranraer Town station where the locomotive could be detached. (*W. S. Sellar*)

112 (opposite below). The snowplough fitted to Stanier 2-6-2 tank No. 40150 is a sign that winter is not considered over yet in the far north at Thurso on Saturday 5 April 1958. The train forming the 3.40 p.m. to Inverness consisted of one container on flat, one fish van, one GW siphon bogie van and two coaches. These would be taken by 40150 as far as Georgemas Junction where they would be attached to the 3.35 p.m. portion from Wick. Leaving Georgemas at 4.15 p.m. behind a pair of Stanier 'Black 5s' the train then consisted of seven coaches and four other vehicles. On reaching Helmsdale, the Restaurant Buffet Car and the Highland Railway Travelling Post Office were attached and Inverness was reached at 9.35 p.m. Pre-war, this train was named 'Orcadian'.

(*Neville Simms*)

114. Traces of snow linger at Crieff on Saturday 12 March 1955 as 'Black 5' No. 45016 awaits departure with the 12.07 p.m. to Gleneagles, use of a tender locomotive obviating the taking of coal at Crieff. The station had been rebuilt in lavish style by the Caledonian Railway in 1893, replacing the original Crieff Junction Railway structure of 1856, but no trace of it remains today.

(*W.A.C. Smith*)

115. At Dunblane, on Saturday 6 August 1960, the empty stock of the 5.35 p.m. local from Glasgow (Buchanan Street) which had, rather surprisingly, arrived hauled by B1 No. 61067 of Parkhead shed to be placed in the goods yard and remain there until Monday morning while the locomotive returned light to Glasgow. However, the local had preceded the late running 5.15 p.m. Buchanan Street to Oban and when the latter arrived 45 minutes down at 7.03 p.m. and hauled by ailing 'Black 5' No. 45470, the B1 was commandeered to provide pilot assistance and, no doubt, a 'cop' for many spotters on the Oban line.   (*W. A. C. Smith*)

116. One of the gas lamps that stood on Dunblane station platform, photographed on Tuesday 31 March 1964. The 'Scottish Central' railway was a section of the main line between Greenhill and Perth opened on 22 May 1848, subsequently taken over by the Caledonian Railway in 1865.   (*Neville Simms*)

119 (above). The sun positioned low down in the sky can create lighting conditions that add drama to a scene, and so it was at Grandtully in November 1957 as Caley 0-4-4 tank No. 55209 makes a vigorous departure from the station watched by local children on the overbridge. The train is the 2.30 p.m. from Ballinluig to Aberfeldy.

(*W. J. V. Anderson – Rail Archive Stephenson*)

117 (opposite above). The mixed train was a familiar sight in Scotland particularly on branch lines where not enough goods traffic was generated all the time to run both passenger and goods trains on a regular basis. At Killin Junction station on Monday 27 April 1961 there is a short burst of activity with the arrival of the 10.03 a.m. train from Killin headed by McIntosh class 2F 'Jumbo' 0-6-0 No. 57441, a pleasant change from the usual Caley 0-4-4 tank.

(*Ron Herbert*)

118 (opposite below). There is a very 1920s feel about this picture at Aberfeldy on Monday 14 May 1928, particularly the clothing style of the ladies, who appear to be well wrapped up for this time of year, but not too well wrapped up to avoid the eye of the fireman who is having a sneaky look out of the cab of McIntosh 0-4-4 tank No. 15215. The tank is attached to the two non-corridor coaches that would convey the ladies to Ballinluig at 5.07 p.m.

(*H. C. Casserley*)

122 (above). Trees were planted around stations exposed to the elements in an effort to provide windbreaks, as seen in this view at Killin Junction on Wednesday 1 August 1951, as Stanier 'Black 5' No. 44957 rolls in with the 5.15 p.m. Oban to Glasgow train. Being purely a junction station, there was no road access and it took the photographer nearly half an hour to clamber up the mountainside from the tiny hamlet of Ardchyle to take this picture, after which he had to clamber down again to retrieve his bicycle. (*Neville Simms*)

120 (opposite above). Having arrived at Callander with the 12.00 noon train from Glasgow Buchanan Street to Oban on Saturday 14 May 1960, Stanier 'Black 5' No. 45443 has drawn the first three coaches off and is shunting them over to the up side of the station. After completing this manoeuvre, the 'Black 5' will pick up its train and proceed on its journey through stunning scenery. Stabled in the bay platform is a 3-car Swindon 'Cross Country' DMU. (*Michael Mensing*)

121 (opposite below). In contrast to the previous picture, Callander station is a place of comparative tranquillity on Saturday 21 August 1954 as Fairburn 2-6-4 tank No. 42199 awaits departure with the 5.45 p.m. train to Stirling. The line and station closed on 1 November 1965, the area now being used for the customary coach and car park. (*W. A. C. Smith*)

123 (left). The photographer found an interesting line-up of ex-Caledonian locomotives at Larbert on the afternoon of Wednesday 23 May 1928. Adjacent to the platform, McIntosh 139 class 3P 4-4-0 No. 14457 pilots McIntosh 49 class 4P 4-6-0 No. 14751. There were only two in the 49 class, this one being named SIR JAMES THOMPSON until the LMS painted over the name. The two locomotives are waiting to proceed southwards with an Aberdeen to Glasgow express. (See caption 124 opposite.) (H. C. Casserley)

125 (above). At this time a motor car was an uncommon sight, here proceeding along the road at Aviemore on Saturday 18 June 1927. The cyclist, however, cannot help but look at the splendid entourage passing him on the railway. Rebuilt Loch class 4-4-0 No. 14379 LOCH INSH and Clan class 4-6-0 No. 14766 CLAN CHATTON, at this time both in LMS livery, make a powerful departure with the 11.00 a.m. Inverness to Glasgow train. The mixture of rolling stock includes two Midland Railway 50-foot luggage composites from St Pancras, an LNWR 50-foot brake, LNWR 57-foot 3rd, LNWR 42-foot 3rd and various other LNWR vehicles.
(H. C. Casserley)

124 (opposite below). On the adjacent track at Larbert on 23 May 1928, a pair of McIntosh Dunaslistair II class 2P 4-4-0s, Nos. 14336 and 14329, wait for a clear road as the train from Aberdeen proceeds on its journey. All the locomotives are fitted with eight-wheel bogie tenders of differing types; No. 14336 has been paired with a larger capacity tender than its classmate. Before the grouping this scene would have been a mass of Caledonian blue with dark brown and white panel carriages, but by this time engines and coaches were LMS red. Adjacent to the gangers stands a classic Caledonian lower quadrant signal with the typically long signal arm.
(H. C. Casserley)

126. The Solway viaduct, around a mile long and some 35 feet above low tide level, spanned the waters of the bleak Solway Firth and connected Bowness-on-Solway in Cumberland with Annan in Scotland's Dumfriesshire. Consisting of 181 single piers with five cast-iron columns in each and 12 double piers, it was constructed during the 1860s. During its relatively short life it was damaged by ice floes, amongst other problems, and was out of use for three years, all of which culminated in its demolition during the mid-1930s. Photographs of the viaduct, especially with a train passing over it, are rare. This one is believed to have been taken prior to the First World War and includes two gentlemen fishing with lines, apparently oblivious to the train rumbling over this impressive structure.

The locomotive is one of two identical 0-6-0 tender engines built by Neilsen & Co in 1868 and purchased by the Solway Junction Railway in 1869, subsequently being taken over by the Caledonian Railway in 1873 and renumbered 381 and 382 (both locomotives were fitted with full length tender hand rails). The mixed train comprises a Caledonian Centre Brake Third, Furness Railway six-wheeler possibly for stockmen, and a mixture of Caledonian sheep trucks and medium-sized cattle wagons.

(*J. G. Gaddes Collection*)

127. Ex-Caley 0-4-4 tank No. 55238 works its way over Connel Ferry Bridge with the 10.48 a.m. Ballachulish to Connel Ferry train on Saturday 22 May 1960. The cantilever bridge is an impressive structure with a clear height of 50 feet above high water level and another 75 feet to the top of each cantilever. The two cantilever piers are founded on rock and the three arched approaches are built of granite. The structure was both a rail and road bridge, the road being only just wide enough for a vehicle, and they were not allowed on the bridge while a train was passing over. Consequently the road was gated and controller by a bridgekeeper who also collected a toll from both foot and vehicle passengers. (For an overall view of the bridge, see illustration 300.)

(*Michael Mensing*)

128 (above). The photographer visited Kirkcudbright on a very dull and overcast Thursday 16 April 1953 where he found class 2P 4-4-0 No. 40577 waiting with the 4.45 p.m. train to Dumfries. The bracket signal was attached to the single road engine shed built tight against the platform. The branch between Castle Douglas and Kirkcudbright was opened in 1864 and closed in May 1965. (*H. C. Casserley*)

130 (above). The standby passenger engine at Ayr after the departure of the resident B1s fell to B.R. Standard 2-6-0 No. 76096 and the engine was frequently used on the summer Saturday train from Heads of Ayr to Edinburgh for which it was kept in sound mechanical condition and a suitable state of cleanliness. On Saturday 24 July 1965 the locomotive works away from Ayr station with the train, as grubby Standard class 5 4-6-0 No. 73104 rolls in with a train from Glasgow to Girvan. (*Derek Cross*)

129 (opposite below). Some of the class 2P 4-4-0 locomotives in Scotland were smartened up by the staff on the sheds, often by painting the door hinges, buffer edges etc. with white paint, but not many were painted as finely as 40573 from Hurlford shed. The locomotive is standing at Kilmarnock station with the 6.05 p.m. train to St Enoch via Dalry on Saturday 28 May 1955. At the adjacent platform 'Black 5' No. 45281 pauses on the 3.08 p.m. Dumfries to Glasgow train. (*John Edgington*)

131. The young ladies in the front compartment of the 4.55 p.m. train to Ballachulish are fascinated by the fact that someone is bothering to photograph their train as it makes a vigorous departure from Oban on Saturday 13 May 1961. The motive power was the usual Caley type 2P 0-4-4 tank, this one No. 55263 built by the LMS and fitted, as were many others, with a less than flattering stovepipe chimney. The station signalbox controlled all movements in the station area, and it was demolished in 1988.

(Michael Mensing)

132. The ladies in the front compartment look somewhat quizzically at the photographer as they pass in the 1.42 p.m. train from Killin to Killin Junction on Wednesday 17 May 1961, hauled by a commendably clean ex-Caley 0-4-4 tank No. 55204. Locomotives had to work hard on the 1 in 50 gradient all the way to Killin Junction, so the local residents no doubt ascertained which way the wind was blowing before hanging out the washing!

(Michael Mensing)

A RETURN TICKET TO SCOTLAND

133. and 134. To quote the photographer's own words, the Campbeltown and Machrihanish light narrow gauge railway on the Mull of Kintyre was the most inaccessible line in the British Isles, needing a whole day to make a visit possible even from Glasgow. He made that journey from Fairlie Pier on Saturday 2 August 1930 and, due to a rough voyage, arrived an hour late at Campbeltown, where he captured these photographs of 1907-built Andrew Barclay 0-6-2 tank ATLANTIC waiting at the quayside with a train for Machrihanish. The 2'-3" gauge line was built primarily to carry minerals, and it was due to lack of goods traffic that the line closed at the end of 1931. *(H. C. Casserley)*

135 & 136. Balloch Pier station on Sunday 14 August 1960 and passengers board P.S. 'Maid of the Loch' at Balloch Pier for a cruise on Loch Lomond. This 555-ton paddle steamer was ordered by the Railway Executive in the summer of 1950 and was built at the Glasgow shipyard of A. & J. Inglis Ltd., then dismantled and transported in sections by rail to Balloch on the loch side, to be re-erected and launched in March 1953. The steamer entered service on 25 May 1953 carrying the British Railways 'lion and wheel' emblem. This was not, so far as we are able to ascertain, carried by any other vessel, and it was removed in 1970. 'Maid of the Loch' became part of the Gourock-based Caledonian Steam Packet Company fleet in 1957. With the numerous reorganisations which plagued British Railways, she was later transferred to the new Scottish Transport Group and then to Caledonian MacBrayne Ltd., but with increasing unreliability and declining passenger numbers, the 'Maid' operated her final cruise on 30 August 1981, and was laid up at Balloch. Since then there has been a long and complicated history of changes in ownership. Eventually purchased by Dumbarton District Council and transferred to a trust, she is now undergoing a slow restoration, currently being used as a floating restaurant, and her massive 1060 NHP steam engine by Rankin & Blackmore is being restored by volunteers, possibly to sail again on the loch at a future date. (*All photographs Ken Fairey*)

137 The 'British Railways' lion and wheel emblem fixed to the bows of 'Maid of the Loch'.

105

138. Largs, birthplace of Alexander Selkirk (Robinson Crusoe) had its station on the picturesque East of Fife line and is seen on Monday 22 April 1957 as D30 4-4-0 No. 62418 THE PIRATE, a not inappropriate name in the area, arrives with the 2.30 p.m. from Crail to Glasgow (Queen Street) and crosses the 2.39 p.m. from Thornton Junction to Crail headed by D34 No. 62468 GLEN ORCHY. The station site is now a car park. (*W. A.C. Smith*)

139. The classic view of Oban station and its surroundings in seen here on the sunny day of Saturday 13 May 1961 as the 4.55 p.m. train to Ballachulish departs from platform 1 behind 0-4-4 tank No. 55263 watched by a mother and daughter. In platform 2 stands the 5.15 p.m. train to Glasgow Buchanan Street and Edinburgh Princes Street headed by a pair of N.B. Loco Co. Diesel Electrics, the front one being No. D6135. On the hill stands McCaig's Tower which was apparently intended to be a replica of the Colosseum in Rome but was never finished and thus ended up as a folly. (*Michael Mensing*)

140. A mile from Killin was Loch Tay station and in 1892 a pier was opened there with an eye on the tourist market and from where steamer services were operated, sailing the loch up to Kenmore, a trip of around 14 miles. At its zenith of popularity a passenger steamship and two goods barges plied the loch but as time progressed only the passenger steamship 'Queen of the Lake' remained, and that was withdrawn from service in 1939. As a consequence Loch Tay station closed on 9 September 1939. The branch was worked from 1890 by Dugald Drummond-designed Caley 0-4-4 tanks until their demise when they were replaced by the McIntosh 0-4-4 tanks. Here at Loch Tay station on Tuesday 28 July 1931 Drummond tank No. 15103 stands with the 1.20 p.m. train to Killin and Killin Junction. In the distance through the summer heat and smoke haze is the small locomotive shed.   (*H. C. Casserley*)

141. Passenger services were withdrawn from the Balerno branch in 1943, but it was still used for goods until 1967 and as a consequence was visited by the District Engineers Department from time to time. At Colinton on Monday 31 July 1961, officers alight from Inspection Saloon No. 970113. This saloon was originally built for Sir Edward Watkin, chairman of the Manchester, Sheffield & Lincolnshire Railway. After their inspections, the saloon was propelled along the branch to Ravelrig Junction by ex–Caley 0-4-4 tank No. 55189. This locomotive has been preserved by The Scottish Railway Preservation Society and restored to original condition with its Caledonian number 419. *(W. S. Sellar)*

142. British Railways Standard class 2-6-4 tank No. 80118 sweeps past an impressive row of vehicles plodding along on the adjacent road near Bishopton with the 12.15 p.m. Gourock to Glasgow Central on Monday 19 April 1965. These standard class 4 tanks tended to monopolise these services after their introduction to traffic in Scotland at the beginning of 1952. This particular example started work at Whitby, transferred to Leeds (Neville Hill) and eventually arrived at Polmadie via Carstairs in 1964.

(*J. C. Beckett*)

143. Stanier 'Black 5' No. 45119 works hard between the curved overgrown platforms of Ardrossan North station, whilst returning a special train to Newcastle-upon-Tyne after connecting with a charter cruise down the Firth of Clyde at Montgomerie Pier on Tuesday 18 August 1959.

The ex-Caledonian station at Ardrossan North closed to local passenger traffic in July 1932 and only witnessed passing passenger trains from then onwards. The old station building with its clock tower still stands and can be seen above the tender of the 'Black 5' between the smoke and safety-valve steam. In the distance, dock cranes at Ardrossan Quay penetrate the skyline.

(*W.A.C. Smith*)

144. It's an all-out thrash on the 1 in 60 gradient up towards Glenoglehead with Caley Jumbo 0-6-0 No. 17466 and Pickersgill 4-6-0 No. 14626 both giving their all with an Edinburgh to Oban special in 1936. This climb was graphically described by O. S. Nock in the January 1939 *Railway Magazine*: "The Ascent to the 940 feet Glenoglehead summit really begins with the tug-of-war on restarting from Balquhidder station. To the thunderous exhaust beats from the engines the train is lifted up the hillside while far below there gradually opens out a fascinating view of Loch Earn. The village of Lochearnhead and the graceful curving viaduct of the railway to Crieff seem but a stone's throw a hundred feet or so down the hillside. The tranquil beauty of this scene is greatly enhanced by the altitude of our travelling viewpoint, (seen in illustration 308). As the prospect of Loch Earn is gradually cut off, the train winds round a spur of the mountain into the wild moraine of Glen Ogle, the engines pound away up the almost impossible ledge cut in the hillside, the tumbling array of vast boulders and look of utter desolation certainly make a picture as savage as it is contrasting with the placid vista of a few moments ago".

(*F. R. Hebron – Rail Archive Stephenson*)

145. A period piece at Achnashellach on Monday 20 June 1927 as Skye Bogie 4-4-0 No. 14283 breasts the top of the 1 in 60 gradient as it works off the single line and into the station with the 4.10 p.m. train from Dingwall to Kyle of Lochalsh. In the opposite platform the safety valves lift on Small Ben No. 14412 BEN AVON waiting with the 4.30 p.m. train from the Kyle. There is no rush for the passengers as the fireman on the 'Ben' has yet to obtain the single line token from the signalman. The first three vehicles on this train are LMS period 1 3rd, H.R. Brake composite, and an L & Y van with sliding roof. Just to the right of 14283's buffer beam is the automatic tablet exchange apparatus but it is not in use on this occasion, while, beyond, the River Carron winds its way towards the loch.

(H. C. Casserley)

A RETURN TICKET TO SCOTLAND

146. One of the handsome Small Ben class 4-4-0s designed by Peter Drummond for the Highland Railway No. 14413 BEN ALLIGAN, built in 1900, stands at Blair Atholl with the 9.30 a.m. train from Perth on Wednesday 16 May 1928. The holes in the front buffer beam for bolting on a snowplough are a reminder as to the severity of Scottish winters.

(*H. C. Casserley*)

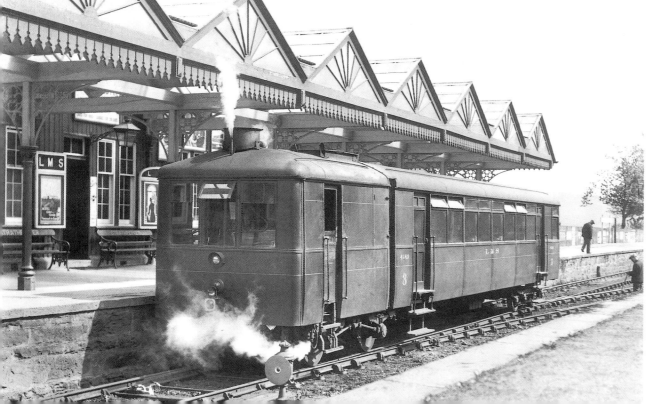

147. In 1928 Henry Casserley visited the Strathpeffer Branch in the hope of seeing the 0-6-0 tank and rake of six-wheeled carriages that had been working the branch in recent times, and would have been none too pleased to find them replaced by a Sentinel railcar. Fortunately, he did deign to photograph car No. 4149 at Strathpeffer after he had arrived with it on the 11.10 a.m. from Dingwall on Friday 18 May. At least it was driven by steam and it's certainly an interesting picture. (*H. C. Casserley*)

148. Not a scrap of litter in sight on this spacious platform at Dornoch, county town of Sutherland and branch terminus, on Saturday 19 May 1928. The footplate crew also looked after their regular branch engine keeping it well cleaned and maintained and the overall appearance is of 'pride in the job'. The branch locomotive for years was one of the four small H. R. Drummond 0-4-4 tanks, in this instance No. 15052 waiting with the 9.00 a.m. train to The Mound. Known locally as 'Dornoch Puggies', No. 55053 became the last working Highland Railway locomotive in service, working the line until its withdrawal in January 1957. The branch closed in June 1960.
(*H. C. Casserley*)

149. This is a very interesting but rather puzzling photograph in the goods yard at Ballachulish during 1935. On a branch where loadings were strictly limited and the normal motive power was nothing larger than ex-Caley 0-4-4 tanks and 0-6-0 goods engines, then what on earth was Pickersgill 191 class 4-6-0 No. 14621 doing at the terminus with an ex-LNWR 50-foot Brake Composite and a 50-foot 3rd in tow, and why were they in the goods yard? Perhaps the grazing sheep have the answer. The station is located behind the trees on the right where the back edge of the near platform can be seen adjacent to the far track.
(*Colling Turner – Rail Archive Stephenson*)

150. The archetypal Highland Railway train stands at Killiecrankie station in the first decade of the 20th century, consisting of locomotive and coaches all designed by David Jones. The locomotive, a Bruce class 4-4-0 heads a four-wheel brake van, six-wheel first lavatory with coupé ends, followed by two six-wheel thirds. All coaches have roof access for inserting oil lamps. The ensemble is awaiting the arrival of a northbound train before it can proceed on its journey along the single track main line.

151. The impressive Ravens Rock cutting situated on the Skye line from Dingwall to Kyle of Lochalsh was the result of an uncooperative landowner who would not let the railway pass through the spa town of Strathpeffer, thus forcing it to take a route further north on a 1 in 50 gradient past Ravens Rock. The Jones Highland Railway 'Sky Bogie' 4-4-0s were built primarily for working this line. Five were constructed with the familiar Jones louvred chimney but the last four built after Jones' retirement had the Drummond chimney from new, as No. 34 built in 1898 and seen here in the cutting with a train from Kyle of Lochalsh during the first decade of the 20th century. Strathpeffer eventually got its own branch line fifteen years after the Dingwall to Strome Ferry line opened in August 1870.

(*Urquhart Dingwall series*)

117

152. This spread of pictures covers two railway tours during 1962 that included the use of preserved Scottish locomotives, the first at Easter named 'The Scottish Rambler', a joint effort between the Stephenson Locomotive Society and The Branch Line Society. The second, in June, called the 'Scottish Rail Tour' was a joint effort between The Railway Correspondence and Travel Society and The Stephenson Locomotive Society. The June tour covered ten days in all and on the evening of Thursday 21 June a trip from Ayr to Kilmarnock and back saw the use of Caley Single 4-2-2 No. 123 from Ayr to Dalry via the Troon goods loop. The locomotive hauled the full tour train of five coaches and despite a strong side wind attained 55 mph between Irvine and Kilwinning. Here we see the locomotive laying an impressive smokescreen while hauling the train at Newton-on-Ayr. It was during this period that No. 123's front buffers had an image of a thistle cleverly etched onto each face.   (*Ray Reed*)

153. Front buffer detail of Caledonian single No. 123.   (*W. S. Sellar*)

154. The Easter tour lasted four days and on Good Friday 20 April 1962 the Caledonian single No. 123 manoeuvres at Kilmarnock after being turned and watered while running a circular tour from Glasgow Central to the Ayr and Muirkirk areas, then returning to Glasgow St Enoch. In the event, the tour ran in the reverse direction, having to improvise on timings and leaving the lineside observers and photographers totally confused. This locomotive with 7'-0" diameter driving wheels was built by Neilson & Co. in 66 days for a cost of £2,600 as a one-off for display at the 1886 Edinburgh Exhibition. In August 1888 it was involved in competition with the East Coast route 'Races to the North' being a regular performer on the West Coast route, running the leg between Carlisle and Edinburgh. *(Neville Simms)*

155. The Scottish Rambler trip on Saturday 21 April 1962 commenced at Inverness, travelled to Keith, taking in the branches to Burghead and Fochabers Town en route before traversing the Great North of Scotland Railways lines and branches, finishing the day at Aberdeen Waterloo. The first leg to Keith ran behind Jones Goods 4-6-0 No. 103 with a 7.30 a.m. start. This turned out to be very wet for those hardy souls gathered on the platform at Inverness who had already travelled up from Glasgow that morning on a service train. *(Neville Simms)*

156 (above). A very pleasant evening at Sanquhar on the old Glasgow & South Western Nith Valley route finds Standard class 5 4-6-0 No. 73100 pulling away from the station with the 6.10 p.m. local from Carlisle to Glasgow St Enoch on Saturday 27 July 1963. On the left is the impressive sight of the old brickworks which have long since been cleared. Sanquhar station was closed in 1965 but has since re-opened, the platforms being provided with the inevitable 'bus shelters'.
(W.A.C. Smith)

158. After acquisition by the Caley in 1893 of the Greenock and Wemyss Bay Railway, which had been opened in 1865, the line was partially doubled and a second tunnel made at Inverkip. The photograph shows Fairburn 2-6-4 tank No. 42144 emerging from the original bore with the 3.30 p.m. from Wemyss Bay to Glasgow (Central) on Tuesday 26 April 1960. Upon electrification the line reverted to single track and the newer tunnel was abandoned. (*W.A.C. Smith*)

157 (opposite below). At Dunrod, on Tuesday 26 April 1960, the signalman holds the single line tablet which it seems the fireman will be taking at some speed. The train is the 5.30 p.m. Wemyss Bay to Glasgow Central hauled by Fairburn 2-6-4 tank No. 42243, the tablet being required for the single line section to Greenock (Upper). However, upon electrification in 1967, the entire branch reverted to single track with Dunrod becoming a passing place (controlled from Paisley). (*W.A.C. Smith*)

159. On the far north route a busy scene from a bygone era is frozen in time as a preponderance of ladies occupy the platform at Golspie station on Friday 17 July 1931. The train about to depart is the 10.20 a.m. from Inverness to Wick being hauled on this day by ex-Highland Castle 4-6-0 No. 14687 BRAHAN CASTLE. Two miles further north was the private station of Dunrobin situated close to Dunrobin Castle, seat of the Duke and Duchess of Sutherland.

(*H. C. Casserley*)

160. At the end of Britain's remotest branch line, Peter Drummond's diminutive Highland 0–4–4 tank No. 15053 stands at Lybster with the 2.20 p.m. to Wick on Saturday 18 July 1931, ready for the 13¾ mile return journey. The first coach No. 18669 is an ex-Highland Railway composite with luggage compartment and four lavatories, built in 1901. The branch, which opened on 1 July 1903, closed entirely on 1 April 1944. *(H. C. Casserley)*

161. A low evening sun creates a dramatic scene on the Highland Railway's single track main line north of Dunkeld as a pair of Hughes/Fowler Mogul 2-6-0s Nos. 13103 and 13101 whistle as they approach Hermitage tunnel with the 3.45 p.m. train from Inverness to Glasgow in the early 1930s. The first vehicle behind the Moguls is an ex-Highland Railway Travelling Post Office No. 10, built in 1916 and used until 1961. This is followed by a WCJS 50-foot composite with central luggage compartment, and then one of the superb C.R. Grampian stock brake composites in which the third class passengers were provided with a standard of comfort comparable with present day 1st class passengers. (*F. R. Hebron – Rail Archive Stephenson*)

Inset. The mileage board displayed outside Wick station in 1931. (H. C. Casserley)

162. Just the sort of wintry conditions you would expect in the north of Scotland prevailed at Wick on Saturday 1 March 1924, and the 2.30 p.m. train from Inverness looks well prepared for a hard journey southwards. The Highland Railway only owned one class of twelve 0-6-0 tender engines. Designed by Peter Drummond, they were nicknamed 'Barneys', this one with the large snow plough and tender sheeting being No. 138. The train engine is a 'Snaigow' class 4-4-0 designed by C. Cumming and built in 1916, of which there were only two. This one fitted with a small wooden plough is No. 74 DURN.

(*L.C.G.B. – Ken Nunn Collection*)

LMS

LONDON EUSTON
729 MILES
CARLISLE 430
GLASGOW 342¼
PERTH 279¼
INVERNESS 161¼
THURSO 20¾
LYBSTER 13¾

MOVING THE GOODS

163. The only coal mine left in the Girvan Valley in March 1965 was the pit at Bargany lying in the Kilgrammie Wood on the main line from Stranraer to Glasgow between Killochan and Dailly. Having negotiated the pit sidings and accessed the main line with a very heavy afternoon coal train, it's an all out thrash for Hughes/Fowler 'Crab' 2-6-0s Nos. 42702 and 42803 as they tackle the 1 in 60 gradient heading for their destination of Ayr Harbour. Behind the train is the pleasant timber-built signalbox that controlled the comings and goings from Bargany sidings.

(*Derek Cross*)

164. At Annbank Junction on Monday 21 March 1966, Standard class 4 2-6-0 No. 76021 hauling a loaded coal train from Knockshinnoch Colliery bound for Ayr Harbour overshot the signal when the driver was unable to bring the train to a halt in time. Unfortunately, a train of empty coal wagons was coming off the Drogan branch and the inevitable collision occurred, happily not a major disaster and the local school children who had just left school for the day found it most entertaining.

(Derek Cross)

165 (left). Having stopped for water at Tain, a goods train of considerable length receives the all clear to proceed southwards on Monday 7 August 1939. As the recipient of the water, Drummond 'Barney' 0-6-0 No. 17693 restarts past the impressive lower quadrant signal. The fireman cranes from his cab and uses the porter on the opposite platform to make contact with the train's guard who is out of sight. (*Les Hanson*)

166 (below). The clouds were grey and menacing at Inverness on Friday 11 August 1939, but they were no match for the exhaust emanating from the chimney of Drummond 'Barney' 0-6-0 No. 17698 as it heads a goods train along the line to Forres. In this busy scene there is goods in abundance, as on the adjacent lines to the south via Daviot where the tracks rise to cross over the Forres lines, Stanier 'Black 5' No. 5461 has charge of another goods while LMS 'Jinty' 0-6-0 No. 7541 shunts yet another rake of wagons.

(*Les Hanson*)

167. At Wilsontown, the signalman helps the guard unload the van of branch goods on Tuesday 16 January 1962, hauled on this day by ex-Caley Pickersgill 3F 0-6-0 No. 57670. No passenger trains had worked the branch for 12 years but the station still looks well kept including the wonderful Caledonian lower quadrant signal already cleared for the train to proceed. The branch, off the main line between Carstairs and Midcalder on the route to Edinburgh, closed completely in 1964, the signalbox being closed a year earlier.

(*W. S. Sellar*)

168. The shunter works in unison with the driver of Jones Skye Bogie 4-4-0 No. 14279 as they carry out shunting manoeuvres at Kyle of Lochalsh on Monday 20 June 1927. Built in 1893, this was one of nine 'Skye Bogies' that were built primarily for working the line. This elevated view shows well the David Jones trademarks of louvered chimney and transversely placed safety valves on the firebox. The louvres in the outer casing of the double skin chimney were designed to create an updraught when running, to lift the exhaust clear of the cab. Unique to Highland Railway locomotives was the fold-down vacuum pipe.

(*H. C. Casserley*)

169. One of David Jones 'Loch' class 4–4–0s that was rebuilt with a Caledonian boiler after the grouping, No. 14392 LOCH NAVER works into Killiecrankie station from the north with a pick up goods on Tuesday 15 May 1928. The occupants of the rather salubrious residence behind the tree were privileged to witness the comings and goings on the Highland main line at close quarters.

(H. C. Casserley)

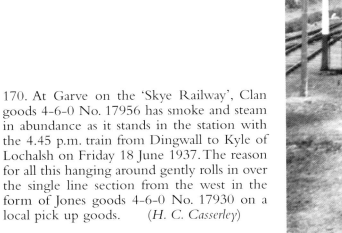

170. At Garve on the 'Skye Railway', Clan goods 4–6–0 No. 17956 has smoke and steam in abundance as it stands in the station with the 4.45 p.m. train from Dingwall to Kyle of Lochalsh on Friday 18 June 1937. The reason for all this hanging around gently rolls in over the single line section from the west in the form of Jones goods 4–6–0 No. 17930 on a local pick up goods.   (H. C. Casserley)

171. There were always rows of assorted wagons standing in sidings at Inverness as here in this view looking out over the Moray Firth on Friday 17 June 1927. On the loading platform is stacked all manner of materials for maintaining the permanent way and from which railwaymen watch Jones Skye Bogie No. 14279 ease its way towards Welsh's Bridge Junction signalbox and the locomotive shed, having been coaled and watered after completing a spell of duty. This was the photographer's first sight of the Highland Railway with its ancient looking locomotives. What a splendid sight it must have been, although by this time the 4-4-0 had exchanged its Highland green livery for LMS red.

(H. C. Casserley)

172. A wonderful panorama at Inverness on Friday 17 June 1927 with rolling stock in abundance from no less than ten different identifiable railway companies, but interestingly there is not a private owner wagon in sight. The locomotive in the foreground manoeuvring an ex-Midland long-wheelbase box van is Highland Railway class 2F 0-6-0 tank No. 16381, one of a class of three known as 'Scrap Tanks' with 5' 2½" driving wheels. They were built with parts from old 2-4-0 tender engines in 1903/4. In the siding above the box van and Caledonian brake composite coach is the bunker end of Stroudly-designed 0-6-0 tank No. 57B LOCHGORM which at this time still retained its Highland Railway identity and dull green livery, while to the left partly obscured by the soot-encrusted tree is the carriage depot. In the foreground a few hundred tons of coal await transportation to the hand-operated coaling stage.

(H. C. Casserley)

173. In the rolling fertile Scottish lowlands at Drumlanrig tunnel, workstained Stanier 'Black 5' No. 44875 is about to dive into the 1410 yard–long bore with an up goods consisting of empty mineral wagons on Wednesday 10 July 1963. Drumlanrig tunnel is situated on the ex-Glasgow & South Western main line between Dumfries and Kilmarnock.

(*Michael Mensing*)

174. On the Caledonian line between Muirkirk and Carstairs, ex–Caledonian McIntosh 3F 0-6-0 No. 57608 puts up an impressive exhaust while climbing the bank out of Inches with the daily goods consisting mainly of mineral wagons on Thursday 10 May 1962. Known as the 812 class, these locomotives were introduced in 1899 and did stirling work throughout their long lives, this one still going strong, and not a sign of a steam leak anywhere, was withdrawn as were the remaining members of the class in the following year.

(*Derek Cross*)

175. The signalman from Throsk walks back to his signalbox after collecting the single line tablet for crossing the Caledonian bridge over the Forth from the driver of ex-Caley Jumbo 2F 0-6-0 No. 57338 heading south towards Alloa with a short container train circa 1957.

    The old driver looking quizzically at the photographer would have seen many changes during his career on the railway and no doubt had numerous tales to tell. He was also well-prepared for any inclement weather, the sheet lying over the cab roof and tied to the handrails could soon be pulled back over the spartan cab and tied to the tender in order to provide added protection for the footplate crew.   *(W. J. V. Anderson – Rail Archive Stephenson)*

176. Motherwell station, rain soaked again, finds an ex-Caley Jumbo 0-6-0 No. 57384 passing through the down main platform with a coal train on Friday 3 August 1962. The elevated disc signal on the opposite platform is a repeater for the up starting signal situated in the cutting at the south end of the station which was partly obscured by the curvature of the platform and an overbridge.

(*R. A. F. Puryer*)

177. Another ex-Caledonian Jumbo No. 57296 brings its brake van out of the smoke-laden tunnel and over the crossover at Stobcross station on the Glasgow Central Low Level line, heading for Stobcross Yard at Queen's Dock on Thursday 23 July 1959. The cylindrical object adjacent to the rail at bottom right was a device activated by the wheel flange for applying grease on curved sections of track (in this case a left hand curve in the direction of Anderston Cross station).

(*W. A. C. Smith*)

178. Working round the curve at Fullwood Junction from the Holytown direction, Hughes/Fowler Mogul 2-6-0 No. 42806 allocated to Ardrossan shed is a long way from home as it heads north through a rain-soaked Mossend station on Friday 3 August 1962. The goods train carries coal from mines in the Holytown, Cleland and Shotts areas and also wagon loads of scrap metal which may well be bound for Glengarnock steelworks in Ayrshire. Mainly known as Moguls in Scotland, these locomotives earned the nickname of 'Crabs' further south in reference to their side-to-side motion when pulling hard.
(R. A. F. Puryer)

179. Friday 3 August 1962 was one of those dull, wet and miserable days in Scotland when the excitement of the long trip north was somewhat tempered by the weather, and it was a case of putting the camera away or adjusting the settings and hoping for the best. Fortunately the photographer chose the latter option and has really caught the mood of the occasion. After observing the really filthy state of Motherwell shed's W.D. 2–10–0 No. 90758, it's probably a good job the sun wasn't shining as it trundled through Motherwell station heading north with a rake of coal empties.   (R. A. F. Puryer)

180. You stand there expecting a tram and instead along Renfrew Road comes a stream locomotive. Such were the sights in Glasgow, this one on Wednesday 26 February 1958. Andrew Barclay 0-4-0 saddle tank (works number 1824, built in 1924) from the Linthouse shipyard of Alexander Stephen & Sons, chugs along the tram tracks of the cobbled road to reach Shieldhall goods station. In the opposite direction, with windows fortunately closed, Glasgow Corporation tram No. 1391 heads for the city.

(*W.A.C. Smith*)

181 (above). South Street, Glasgow, with veteran Caley 'Pug' No. 56029 shunting the Whiteinch Tramway which originated in the 1870s as a privately owned line serving industrial establishments along the north bank of the river. Street running brought the inevitable encounters with impatient motorists as seen here on Thursday 12 June 1958. (*W.A.C. Smith*)

182 (left). Caley 'Pug' 0-4-0 saddle tank No. 56029 is seen again this time at Ibrox making for home after a day's work on Wednesday 26 August 1959. Because of the totally inadequate space for storing coal, a tender has been fashioned out of an old wooden wagon on which the fireman is riding. The low evening sun highlights the basic cab and shows the hole cut out in the cab backsheet for shovelling coal onto the footplate. (*P. Hay*)

183. Low early morning sun creates a dramatic spectacle at Bedlay Colliery on the morning of Thursday 23 April 1981 as the 6 o'clock shift begins. Smoke and steam from the NCB Barclay 'pug' No. 6 hangs in the still frosty atmosphere and contrasts strongly with the trail of smoke from the chimney of the weighbridge hut under the shadow of the huge slagheap looming in the background. Full wagons of coal on the left of the picture will soon be shunted to the weighbridge and weighed before the first trip of the day down the half-mile branch to the B.R. exchange sidings.

(*Joe Rajczonek*)

Bedlay Colliery was situated in rural Scottish countryside some seven miles north-east of Glasgow near Glenboig village. It was quite unique in that the colliery railway system was split between a long charming scenic branch line and a heavily industrial area that had all the paraphernalia of a typical colliery yard with buildings, pit-head gears, slag heaps and huge areas of black coal mud! The other big attraction to the railway photographer was the fact that this was an all steam worked colliery and remained so to the end of its working life. And, if this was not enough, even the locomotive crews were sociable and provided unofficial footplate rides and plenty of smoke for photographs, not to mention the very welcome cup of hot tea in the weighbridge hut on those freezing cold winter days. Its final closure at the end of 1981 was not only a sad loss to the industry but also to the many enthusiasts that once visited the colliery.

184. A bird's eye view of part of the branch line at Bedlay Colliery shows the rural aspect of the surroundings and the weighbridge hut, located near the locomotive where many railway enthusiasts spent hours in between workings and sheltering from the usual adverse weather conditions. Winter sunshine dramatically highlights the coal wagons as NCB No. 17, a four-coupled saddletank built by Andrew Barclay of Kilmarnock in 1952, shunts them towards the back of the colliery ready for loading. Another rake of wagons await their turn in the adjacent sidings on this very busy morning shift at the colliery on Thursday 12 November 1981. There is hardly any indication that within 6 weeks mounting geological problems underground would mean that the colliery would sadly close and so end the only regular NCB steam in Scotland.

(*Joe Rajczonek*)

185. Overnight snow still coats the tops of wagons and tracks as the thaw sets in creating the atmospheric misty conditions during shunting operations at the B.R. exchange sidings at Bedlay Colliery on Friday 6 March 1981. NCB Barclay No. 17 (works No. 2296 built in 1952) stands smoking profusely while the shunter performs his duties coupling up the empty wagons that have just arrived. Once loaded at the colliery these will return down the branch and join the waiting full wagons of coal destined for Ravenscraig Steelworks.

(*Joe Rajczonek*)

186. Following many hours of rain the sun finally makes a brief appearance to highlight the steam from both slag heap and NCB Barclay No. 17 at Bedlay Colliery on Thursday 29 October 1981; an amazing example of how enough heat is generated inside the slag heap to cause the rain water to start steaming in very cold weather conditions and shows the dangerous unstable nature of the slag heap. However, the view of shunting operations taking place from the top of this particular slag heap was extremely interesting and photographically very rewarding. All empty coal wagons once weighed would have been shunted up a severe gradient to this part of the colliery so that they could then be shunted by gravity to the screens and loaded up. (*Joe Rajczonek*)

A RETURN TICKET TO SCOTLAND

Polkemmet Colliery was situated on the edge of Polkemmet Moor south of the town of Whitburn midway between Glasgow and Edinburgh. In the 1970s the railway system at the colliery always had the appearance of being run down with bits and pieces of redundant locomotives scattered around the shed area. Even the locomotives that were serviceable looked very dirty and on their last legs. However, Polkemmet was renowned for double-headed trains and the steam engines literally thrashed up the 1 in 34 mile-long branch to the B.R. exchange sidings. Normally only the morning shift operated and work would be crammed into two busy periods. Sometimes as many as five trips came up the bank in a 90 minute period and each one just as dramatic and noisy as the last. Alas the steam engines gradually became more and more unreliable and once a diesel arrived in 1979 it soon took over all duties and steam working sadly ended.

187. Giesl Ejector fitted NCB Barclay No. 8 of 1912 vintage makes a rare single-headed trip up the branch with a train of full coal wagons for the exchange sidings on Bank Holiday 28 August 1978. With the other steam locomotive out of action the crew take the opportunity to hide away and relax by the side of the weighbridge hut conveniently hidden from the main colliery buildings in the background. Empty wagons can be seen waiting under the colliery screens ready for loading while the pit head gear stands proud.

(*Joe Rajczonek*)

188. Scottish industrial locomotives were affectionately known as 'pugs' and two can be seen in this picture hard at work at Polkemmet Colliery on Wednesday 30 May 1979. NCB Barclays No. 25 (works No. 2358 of 1954) pilots No. 8 (works No. 1296 of 1912) past the huge complex of colliery buildings with a train of freshly mined coal heading for the B.R. exchange sidings. (*Joe Rajczonek*)

189. At Oban on Thursday 18 May 1961, ex-Caledonian 0-4-4 tank 55124 carries out shunting manoeuvres adjacent to the station and railway pier. Never ones to miss a trick, the shunters hitch a ride on the side of the brake van as the stock is drawn out, the rear three vehicles of which are fish vans. In the siding at the end of the building stands one of the former Pullman cars, used as refreshment coaches on the Scottish Region. (*Michael Mensing*)

191 (opposite below). Ex-C.R. 0-6-0 tank No. 56361 trundles past Clan and Blue Funnel Line cargo ships berthed in Glasgow's King George V Dock on 13 March 1956. This, situated between Shieldhall and Renfrew, was opened in 1931 as a planned expansion of Glasgow's already extensive system of docks but, with the advent of containerisation and bulk carriers, it is one of only two docks surviving on the upper Clyde. (*W. A. C. Smith*)

190 (above). At Oban on Thursday 27 July 1961, 0-4-4 tank No. 55204 busies itself shunting wagons on the railway pier, alongside the docked T.S. 'King George V'. This 985 ton steamer was built in 1926 for Turbine Steamers Ltd. by Wm. Denny & Bros. Ltd. of Dumbarton (the builders of the 'Cutty Sark') for service between Greenock and Inveraray. In 1935, ownership was acquired jointly by the LMS railway and David MacBrayne Ltd. And thereafter 'King George V' sailed out of Oban for the latter company. During the Second World War, she made several trips to the Dunkirk beaches in May 1940. 1946 found her sailing on the Greenock to Ardrishaig service, thereafter returning to the seasonal Oban–Staffa–Iona and Fort William–Oban tourist sailings (being laid up on the Clyde in winter) until 1974 by which date she was under Caledonian MacBrayne Ltd. control. After lying at Cardiff for several years, she was in course of conversion into a floating restaurant when gutted by fire. A sad end for a fine steamer. (*J. S. Whiteley*)

192 (above). Four and a half miles north of Beattock station and it's still over five miles to the summit for Stanier 'Black 5' No. 45259 and Fairburn 2-6-4 tank No. 42214 giving their all on the 1 in 75 gradient as they thrash past a coniferous plantation with a heavy northbound goods on Saturday 4 July 1964. A scene that had been repeated countless times since the line opened in 1848, but not for much longer using steam traction. (*Michael Mensing*)

193 (right). Two miles from Connel Ferry an up goods train headed by Stanier 'Black 5' No. 45159 drifts through the countryside towards Taynuilt on Saturday 21 May 1960. In the distance Loch Etive winds its way inland through a landscape for which the Callander and Oban is renowned. (*Michael Mensing*)

194. On Wednesday 29 July 1931, the safety valves of Fowler 4F 0-6-0 No. 4312 lift impatiently while being held with a northbound goods on Killiecrankie viaduct. It is waiting for a southbound train to enter the station on the other side of the tunnel where there is a passing loop. This excellent viewpoint from over the tunnel entrance shows the goods with a Highland Railway brake van bringing up the rear. These brake vans were completely enclosed against the weather with a raised glazed section in the centre of the roof from which the guard could look out. Through the well–wooded Pass of Killiecrankie, the River Garry flows over 50 feet below the railway track.

(*H. C. Casserley*)

195. The approach to the south end of Kilmarnock station has a deceptively rural appearance where the tracks from the station converge to two lines as they pass over the masonry viaduct carrying the railway through the old part of town and over the Marnock River. On Saturday 4 August 1962, long-time resident of Corkerhill Shed Glasgow, ex-Midland Fowler 4F 0-6-0 No. 43899 enters the station during the heat of a summer's day and takes the through line with a northbound train of empty bolster wagons.

(R. A. F. Puryer)

196 (opposite above). Despite the overcast day and freezing cold wind, the sun smiled on the photographer by breaking through the cloud on Monday 3 April 1961 to illuminate this peaceful but busy scene at Ballinluig. On the main line, Stanier 'Black 5' No. 44796 shunts wagons in the station and small goods yard while BR Standard 2-6-4 tank No. 80093 waits to marshal some of the goods wagons onto the rear of the Aberfeldy branch train while awaiting a main line connection. The ensemble would then be worked back to the terminus as a mixed train.

(R. A. F. Puryer)

197 (left). Looking out from the road bridge towards the rock-cutting entrance to Kyle of Lochalsh on Thursday 3 August 1950 finds Clan Goods 4-6-0 No. 57951 departing with a goods for Dingwall. 'The Skye Railway' was home to most of these engines at this time and they could be seen on passenger as well as goods trains. The early morning (summer) Boat Train, 5.05 a.m. from Kyle of Lochalsh non-stop to Dingwall was a favourite, and this connected with the 12.30 a.m. Mail Steamer sailing from Stornaway. Before the Second World War, this train was named 'The Lewisman'.

(*Neville Simms*)

198. After the mist cleared near Lamington in the Clyde Valley, the overnight frost lingered during the day and it was bitterly cold, in fact ideal conditions for observing superb exhausts from steam locomotives. And so it was on Saturday 11 February 1961 as B.R. Clan pacific No. 72000 CLAN BUCHANAN swept by on a down fitted goods. The permanent way workers in their efforts to keep warm hardly notice the spectacle. (*Derek Cross*)

199 (above). Viewed from Perth shed yard, the shadow of Stanier 'Black 5' No. 44721 on the adjacent coaches precedes the locomotive as it works south past its home shed with a mixed goods on Thursday 2 August 1962. Highlighted by the low evening sun as the day draws to a close, the 'Black 5's' crew prepare for a night's work. *(R. A. F. Puryer)*

200 (right). On Friday 4 August 1922, F. G. Smith's River class 4-6-0 No. 940 storms past St Rollox while heading the 7.00 p.m. express goods to Carlisle. Designed for the Highland but bought by the Caledonian Railway, they proved to be the most powerful 4-6-0s on the Caley and after the grouping frequently worked over the parts of the Highland system they were designed for, making a mockery of the Highland Railway's Chief Mechanical Engineer's decision to ban their use due to excess axle loading.
(LCGB – Ken Nunn Collection)

201. The cry of gulls filled the air at Kyle of Lochalsh as the rain fell from a leaden sky on Tuesday 16 August 1960, but when you have travelled a long way you cannot let a few drops of rain get in the way of photography. Suitably dressed for the occasion, railway employees go about their work with an ex-Caledonian McIntosh/Pickersgill 0-4-4 tank No. 55227 on shunting manoeuvres. Photographs exist from around this period showing locomotives working here with H20 and H21 Target numbers on the top lamp bracket, but what these refer to we have been unable to ascertain.   (*Ken Fairey*)

202. Early morning sunlight from an otherwise overcast sky highlights certain aspects of the scene at Kyle of Lochalsh on the not so often photographed east side of the station in the early 1950s. The station pilot, ex–Caledonian McIntosh 0-4-4 tank No. 55216 busies itself shunting goods wagons against a backdrop of mountains on the Isle of Skye as the coal fires are made up in the station building at the start of another day.

(Eric Treacy – N.R.M. ET-LS-F-2869)

WORKERS AND OBSERVERS

203. Clan Goods 4-6-0 No. 17956 shunts wagons of timber stakes at Achnashellach on Friday 18 June 1937 while working a pick up goods. The Clan Goods, designed by Cumming, were essentially a development of the Jones Goods built 23 years earlier but incorporating modern developments and very good engines they were too, although the class only numbered eight locomotives. They were used extensively on the Kyle line. On the platform stands the unusual sight of a 'Wellington' class steam tractor, built by Foster & Co., on 14 June 1920, works No. 14452, licensed to James Armstrong of Inverness, which appears to be under repair.

(H. C. Casserley)

204 (above). An ex-Caledonian 'Beetlecrusher' 0-6-0 tank No. 56168 works past the coaling stage at Dawsholm with an LMS Goods Brake Van while carrying out shunting manoeuvres on Monday 15 August 1960. Their nickname had been earned from their heavy and powerful appearance, especially when compared with their 0-4-0 counterparts. These sturdy little tanks were designed primarily for work on the docks, hence the very short wheelbase for negotiating tight curves.   (Ken Fairey)

205 (right). A quiet moment at Oban on Saturday 14 May 1960 as ex-Caley 2P 0-4-4 tank No. 55238 waits for a path to shunt the empty stock of the 3.57 p.m. train from Ballachulish out of the station, giving the local railwaymen plenty of time to discuss the matters of the day. The station itself, part of which can be seen on the right, was aesthetically very pleasing to the eye, designed in a Swiss chalet style of architecture complete with clock towers (seen in the distance on illustration 282). After shunting out the stock and running round its train, 55238 would then push the carriages back into one of the platforms to form the return train to Ballachulish.   (Michael Mensing)

206. Not the ideal place to stop when you have got the blower full on but it certainly makes for an impressive photograph at Carstairs on Monday 4 September 1961 with BR Clan pacific No. 72002 CLAN CAMPBELL providing the performance. Meanwhile the driver glances back to see what the hold-up is as he waits to get a Glasgow to Manchester train under way. It's hard to believe looking at the condition of 'Clan Campbell' that just over twelve months later this Polmadie-based Clan pacific would be withdrawn from service along with the depot's other four members of the class. (*Tim Mills*)

207 (right). On Friday 4 November 1955, one of the Glasgow Central pilots, Caley 0-4-4 tank No. 55220 had been derailed all wheels outside the station and the Polmadie breakdown train arrived in the charge of standard 2-6-4 tank No. 80027. The crane, R51071/30 and of 30 tons capacity, was built by Ransomes & Rapier in 1942 for the LMS at a cost of £6,000. As both bridges over the Clyde, the original of 1879 and the second (made necessary by enlargement of the station) completed in 1905, were still operational at this time, traffic in and out of the station was not seriously affected. (*W.A.C. Smith*)

208 (below). Five discuss the situation, one watches from the footplate while two do the work, or so it seems at Edinburgh Princes Street station, or perhaps the Caley gangers are discussing the pros and cons of working for the LMS. In this mid-1920s scene, the grouping has taken place even though the Drummond 'Jumbo' 2F 0-6-0 still retains its Caledonian number plate 333, it would be renumbered by the LMS 17432 and then 57432. Forming the backdrop is Lothian Road goods depot.

A RETURN TICKET TO SCOTLAND

209 (right). On Monday 20 July 1931, a representative of the Royal Mail stands at Tomatin station waiting to deposit his bag of mail onto the 1.30 p.m. train from Glasgow to Inverness, a scene that would be repeated at many other stations along the line. Motive power hauling the 1.30 p.m. on this day was Hughes/Fowler Mogul 2-6-0 No. 13102 which is acting as pilot engine to an ex-Highland Railway Castle class 4-6-0. (*H. C. Casserley*)

211. Stanier 'Black 5' No. 45366 simmers at the platform end after arriving at Oban station with the 7.50 a.m. from Glasgow Buchanan Street on Thursday 27 April 1961. As the last of the arriving passengers disperse and mail bags are loaded into the adjacent mail van, the cleaners go to work on the inside of the carriages prior to the stock being shunted out. In the meantime, the footplateman and porter are in deep discussion. *(Ron Herbert)*

210 (opposite below). On Thursday 27 August 1959, Pickersgill ex-C.R. 4-4-0 No. 54470 runs into Kildary with the 12.05 p.m. local from Tain to Inverness and crosses 'Black 5' No. 45461 on the 10.40 a.m. from Inverness to Wick and Thurso. The ex-LNER buffet car in the latter train will come off at Helmsdale for attachment to a southbound service. In this everyday scene, a postman waits to load the mail and a porter has boxes of flowers bound for Forres, as they exchange greetings with the footplatemen. It does not appear that Kildary will be generating much revenue from passengers on this trip. *(W. A. C. Smith)*

212. A busy scene at South Renfrew on Tuesday 2 July 1957 as road users and pedestrians wait at the level crossing gates for McIntosh 3F 0-6-0 No. 57579 to roll into the station with the 5.23 p.m. train from Fulbar Street to St Enoch on which the driver and fireman have momentarily had their attention distracted by something along the road. Simmering directly below, ex-LMS 2P 4-4-0 No. 40642 waits to depart for Renfrew Wharf.

(*H. C. Casserley*)

213. On 10 February 1896, Messrs. G. & G. Thomson Ltd., shipbuilders of Clydebank, purchased from stock a Neilson standard 0-4-0 saddle tank (4919/96). Sixty-two years later, and now John Brown & Co. Ltd. No. 2, it was photographed crossing the tram tracks in Glasgow Road to enter the shipyard, birthplace of the Cunard 'Queens', with plate wagons from Clydebank (West) goods station, on Wednesday 26 February 1958. (*W.A.C. Smith*)

214. A view from the footbridge at Killin Junction station as the sun breaks through a cloudy sky finds Caley type 2P 0-4-4 tank No. 55263 running round its train after arrival with the 1.41 p.m. train from Killin on Monday 16 May 1960. Following the arrival of the connecting train and the transferring of passengers, and goods being wheeled round by the porters, the branch train will depart around the curve past the signalbox and down the 1 in 50 gradient back to Killin; a once typical scene that was repeated countless times at this junction station until its closure in September 1965. (*Michael Mensing*)

215 (above). Even as early as 1952, the glazed overall station roof at Oban leaked in a number of places, as the puddles on the platform bear witness on Saturday 19 April. For the porters and passengers it's just another inconvenience as they go about their business, well wrapped up against the inclement weather. An example of past skills can be seen in the elaborate fascia around the stationmaster's office. (H. C. Casserley)

216 (right). The photographer's suitcases have been well secured against springing open as they wait on the platform at Gourock for their owner to photograph B.R. Standard class 5 4-6-0 No. 73061 on Thursday 5 September 1963, the locomotive that had hauled the train from Glasgow, while the porter assists a lady with her luggage. From Gourock, steamers sailed to a number of destinations, from the short crossing to Dunoon to the longer trips to the Isle of Arran, to Campbeltown on Kintyre, and Inveraray.

(Alistair Nisbett)

217. One of the more unusual sights which appears to have been unique to Scotland's railways was the practice of the driver or fireman being out on the running plate of their locomotive carrying out various jobs while the train was in motion, even though this was forbidden by the railway authorities. Here the driver of McIntosh 'Dunalastair IV' 4-4-0 No. 925 appears to be carrying out front end lubrication while pounding up Beattock with his train, just prior to the First World War. Interestingly the train is running with one headlamp and no Caledonian 'bow tie' route indicator even though the roof boards on the carriages suggest it to be a principal express, the first vehicle of which is an LNWR Full Brake.

(H. Gordon-Tidy)

218 (left). In the bay platform at Muir of Ord station on Wednesday 10 April 1946, Small Ben 4-4-0 No. 14406 BEN SLIOCH backs onto a Caledonian Corridor Brake Composite coach that will form the 3.35 p.m. service to Fortrose. Passenger services on the branch were withdrawn on 1 October 1951 although a Camping Coach remained in use at Fortrose for a number of years after. Goods traffic continued on the branch until June 1960. (*H. C. Casserley*)

219 (below). While awaiting the arrival of trains on the Highland single track main line, there was plenty of time to carry out locomotive maintenance in the passing loops situated at stations along the route. In the quiet rural setting of Blair Atholl on Tuesday 15 May 1928, the driver passes the time of day on the front of McIntosh 3F 0-6-0 No. 17633 while waiting to proceed southwards with a goods train consisting of freshly hewn timber. (*H. C. Casserley*)

220. On the main line between Edinburgh and Carstairs during February 1963, a down goods became stuck in snowdrifts near Cobbinshaw. A snow plough was sent from Edinburgh to clear the route, hauled by two Stanier 'Black 5s' and a class 4MT tank, and this also became stuck close to the abandoned goods train. A second snow plough was made up at Carstairs consisting of three Stanier 'Black 5s' and here we see the second plough being re-arranged in preparation to pull out the first on Sunday 10 February 1963. The goods train had by this time already been pulled clear on the Friday.

(*Stuart Currie*)

221. Backing up for a mile and then charging snowdrifts up to 15 feet deep with three 'Black 5s' at 50 m.p.h. all with whistles sounding a general warning must have been an amazing experience. Add to this the fact that the footplate crews could not see through the mass of snow being hurled around, it must have been unnerving even for the most resolute of footplatemen. (*Stuart Currie*)

222. The second plough was fitted with full length snow ploughs either end of the three 'Black 5s'. The bottom of the plough was situated around four inches above rail level. When ploughing, the spring-loaded plough was pushed down by the pressure of the snow until its front edge actually slid along the top of the running rails. These large ploughs restricted visibility from the footplate.
(*Stuart Currie*)

223. After clearing the down line near Wilsontown Junction on Friday 8 February 1963, the triple engine snow plough attempted to clear the up line on the Saturday. Unfortunately the uneven side thrust due to a wall of snow on one side and a clear track on the other, plus the fact that the plough had been slowed right down by the snow, caused the rear driving wheels on the leading engine to derail, bringing proceedings to an abrupt halt. Here railwaymen discuss the situation as they await the arrival of the Breakdown Gang from Carstairs. (*Stuart Currie*)

224 (above). With all permanent way men and other personnel cleared away from the vicinity of the track, the three 'Black 5s' smash into the 10 feet deep snowdrift at speed. The shape of the plough forces the snow upwards out of the cutting as they tackle the section towards Cobbinshaw on Sunday 10 February.   (*Stuart Currie*)

225 (right). The snowploughs were assisted by many permanent way men, a number of whom are digging out the up line near Wilsontown Junction in readiness for the Breakdown Gang who had arrived to re-rail the 'Black 5' seen in the background.
(*Stuart Currie*)

226. David Jones 'Skye Bogie' 4-4-0 No. 14277 is in pristine external condition and looked splendid in lined out LMS red livery while being turned on the 50-foot diameter Muir of Ord turntable in readiness to work the 3.50 p.m. train to Fortrose on Monday 21 May 1928. The table was not vacuum fitted to assist rotation so it's "shoulders to it" for the footplate crew. In the siding stands a veteran coach in use by the Engineers' Department.

(*H. C. Casserley*)

227. Since the photograph in illustration 226 was taken, the rails on Muir of Ord turntable have been extended over the pit wall to accommodate larger locomotives such as the Clan Goods 4-6-0 No. 57954 seen here on Tuesday 8 August 1950. Even so, the engine only just fits the table, making it difficult to balance and hard work to turn round, and even the help from a young boy was welcome. This locomotive had been fitted with a Caledonian superheater relief or 'snifting' valve to the rear of the chimney from where the steam is emanating. The Clan was being prepared for the 5.40 p.m. mixed train to Fortrose, the regular branch engine being at Inverness shed for boiler washout. (*Neville Simms*)

228. At Fortrose, terminus of the Black Isle Branch from Muir of Ord, it's "shoulders to the bar" again, as this 50-foot diameter turntable was not vacuum fitted either. On Wednesday 10 April 1946, Small Ben 4-4-0 No. 14406 BEN SLIOCH is turned after working the 3.35 p.m. train from Muir of Ord. A very pleasant sight to have at the end of your garden for any enthusiasts living in the adjacent dwellings! (*Richard Casserley*)

175

229 (right). The driver and fireman obviously found the photographer and his plate camera a bit of a novelty at Balquhidder on Saturday 11 June 1927 while replenishing the water tanks of McIntosh 0-4-4 tank No. 15159. The locomotive arrived at 6.55 p.m. on a train from Crieff and after running round was due to depart on the return train at 7.30 p.m.
(H. C. Casserley)

230 (below). There is plenty of time for the driver and fireman of Stanier 'Black 5' No. 45214 to exchange local gossip with the signalman at Taynuilt on Tuesday 17 May 1960. The goods train consisted of ten Presflo Alumina wagons from Burntisland en route to Ballachulish and the British Aluminium Works at Kinlochleven and was being held at Taynuilt while waiting for an up goods to pass. (Michael Mensing)

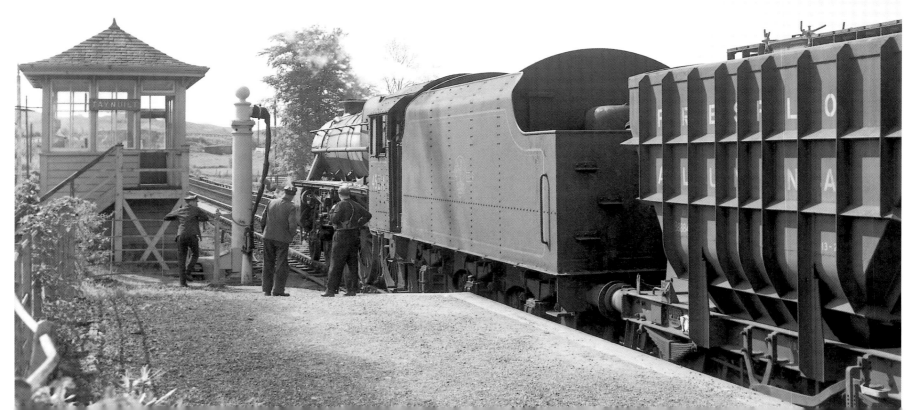

231. 'One man and his dog' watch proceedings at Helmsdale as Stanier 'Black 5' No. 45496 takes on water prior to detaching the TPO and Restaurant Car from the 11.05 a.m. Inverness to Wick train on Tuesday 8 September 1959. Three vertical-boarded wooden Travelling Post Offices were built in 1916 to carry the greatly increased volume of mail to the Royal Navy base at Scapa Flow and they continued working right through to 1961.   (*Brian Stephenson*)

232 (below). The automatic tablet exchange apparatus designed by James Manson when he was Locomotive Superintendent of the Great North of Scotland Railway in the late 1880s has been well photographed here just at the moment of exchange at Brora on the Highland main line. With this apparatus, tablets could be exchanged safely at speeds in the high 70s, whereas the manual hoop exchange speed was limited by the risk of personal injury to the fireman or signalman. In this view, a short goods train from Inverness to Wick rattles past the south end of the station behind Stanier 'Black 5' No. 44998 on Monday 1 August 1960. (*Brian Stephenson*)

233 (above). Stanier 'Black 5' No. 45423 and an unidentified classmate ease off after reaching the summit of the climb from Oban with the 5.15 p.m. train to Glasgow Buchanan Street and Edinburgh Princes Street on Monday 16 May 1960. The manual hoop, the pouch of which contains the tablet, is about to be exchanged at Glencruitten crossing box, thus enabling the trains to enter the next section of single line track. (*Michael Mensing*)

234. At Invershin on Thursday 10 August 1939 an ex-Highland Railway Drummond 'Barney' 0-6-0 No. 17703 pilots Stanier 'Black 5' No. 5009 as they work purposefully through the station with a northbound goods, the low platform height emphasizing the size of the locomotives. Both locomotives are fitted with Manson's automatic tablet exchange apparatus. On the 0-6-0 the fork has been raised suggesting that the token has just been collected from the lineside apparatus, although tokens would normally be exchanged by the train engine and not the pilot.   (*Les Hanson*)

235. "You could only spend this sort of honeymoon with a railway enthusiast!" You can imagine Henry Casserley's wife Kathleen thinking that as she sits somewhat wearily on the platform seat at Killiecrankie after climbing to a position over the tunnel entrance with her husband in order to obtain (amongst others) the photograph shown in this book as illustration 194. Still at least there is the chance of a breather while waiting for the 12.15 p.m. Perth to Blair Atholl train seen rolling in behind one of the excellent Jones Goods 4-6-0s No. 17919 on Wednesday 29 July 1931.   (*H. C. Casserley*)

236 (opposite above). Despite its dilapidated appearance, Renfrew Wharf survived until closure of the branch in 1967. It was used by workers at neighbouring industrial establishments which included two small shipyards, hence its very restricted timetable. The power station in the background was that at Yoker, on the opposite (north) bank of the Clyde but is now demolished, while the embankment just visible in front of the tenements on the left carried the Central Low Level line. On Monday 11 June 1956, locomotive and crew patiently await departure time with the 6.08 p.m. train to Glasgow St Enoch, headed by Fowler 2P 4-4-0 No. 40596.   (*Dick Thompkins – Ken Fairey Collection*)

237 (below). There is certainly no rush of passengers at Leith North on Saturday 24 July 1954 and with it being a very pleasant morning there is no point hanging about in the hot cab of a locomotive. Quite sensibly the driver elects to spend a few minutes relaxing on the platform seat prior to departing with ex-Caley 0-4-4 tank No. 55165 and the 8.54 a.m. train to Edinburgh Princes Street. The branch to Leith North was closed at the end of April 1962. *(John Edgington)*

OBAN

BALLACHULISH

Opposite sides of a British Railways-era carriage destination board.

238. Before the boom in road transport, rural branch lines were linked into the way of life for the people along their routes, acting as their main means of transport and where they frequently exchanged information and gossip, whilst also providing a lifeline to the outside world for the goods which enabled them to make a living. As an added bonus the railway provided local employment opportunities. Here at Benderloch on a rain and wind-swept Saturday 19 April 1952 is the briefest glimpse of what the branch lines were all about, as inhabitants from this rural farming and crofting community make for the station exit, having been into Oban for some weekend shopping. Friendly goodbyes are waved as the 12.30 p.m. train from Connel Ferry prepares to continue along the 28 mile branch towards the terminus at Ballachulish, a once familiar scene between the years 1905 and 1966. (*H. C. Casserley*)

239. 'Black 5' No. 45359 passes Drumvaich loop with the 1.18 p.m. from Callander to Glasgow (Buchanan Street) on 11 September 1965. This passing place was installed by the Caledonian in 1893 on the former Dunblane, Doune and Callander Railway. In 1902 the line was doubled from Dunblane to Doune (it reverted to single track in 1955) and the intention was to complete this to Callander, but this was never done and Drumvaich remained a passing place until closure of the line late in 1965. Similar signal box/house combinations were to be seen at St Brides, Glenlochy and Glencruitten on the Oban line. In 1955 the signal box at Drumvaich was manned from 6.00 a.m. to 11.25 p.m. Monday to Friday and from 5.05 a.m. on Saturday to 1.00 a.m. on Sunday.

(*W.A.C. Smith*)

240. The clean lines of Pickersgill class 3P 4-4-0 No. 54470 show up in the afternoon sun at Inverness station on Monday 14 September 1959. With everything prepared for departure on the locomotive, driver and fireman put the world to rights with a member of the public while awaiting departure time with the 3.14 p.m. stopping train to Tain. Built by the Caledonian, the whole class of 48 locomotives were still in service with the advent of British Railways in 1948, and the last member of the class was not withdrawn until 1963.

(*Brian Stephenson*)

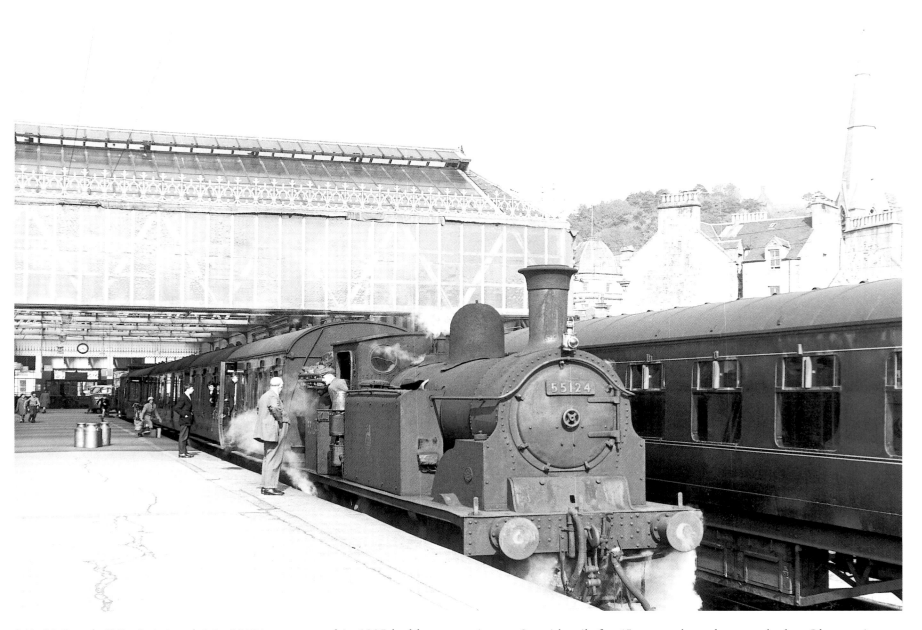

241. McIntosh C.R. 0-4-4 tank No. 55124 constructed in 1895 had been running on Scottish rails for 65 years when photographed at Oban station on Thursday 27 April 1961 during its last year in service. Under the overall roof, passengers board the train for Ballachulish as the hands of the clock move to 4.40 p.m., fifteen minutes to departure time, so there was plenty of time for a chat with the driver. This really impressive station was demolished in 1987. A far more mundane new facility had been opened for the people of Oban in January 1986.

(*Ron Herbert*)

242. Branch line stations are very quiet places for most of the time but with the arrival of a train the place suddenly comes to life with passengers and railway employees all going about their business. Surrounded by all the paraphernalia that adorned platforms after being unloaded from the train, the station staff at Killin busy themselves sorting it all out on Monday 22 June 1953. Gently simmering at the platform edge with the 1.42 p.m. train to Killin Junction, ex-Caley 0-4-4 tank No. 55222 completes this idyllic scene. Local people always referred to the conveyance as "the Wee Train".

(*B. K. B. Green – Initial Photographs*)

243 (opposite above). Having arrived at Aberfeldy with the 1.02 p.m. mixed train from Ballinluig on Monday 23 May 1955, the footplate crew take the opportunity to clean out the cab and oil up ex-Caley 0-4-4 tank No. 55212 while the station staff prepare to unload the train. The locomotive will then run round its train and shunt the three wagons of coal and a brake van into the goods yard before coupling up to the coach for the return journey of 8¾ miles to Ballinluig. The coach is one of the rare 60-foot Period 1 vehicles rebuilt as a Brake Composite with Stanier sides, while retaining the original roof and underframes. Of the six daily workings on this branch, three were allowed to be mixed trains in the Working Timetable. (*W.A.C. Smith*)

244 (left). Passengers shelter under the canopy while others prepare to board the train at a very wet Aberfeldy station on Friday 23 July 1954. Due out at 1.45 p.m. the motive power is ex-Caley 0-4-4 tank No. 55218. Locomotives working at the branch were provided by Perth and sub shedded at Aberfeldy until the branch's closure on 3 May 1965.

(*John Edgington*)

DOWN AT THE LOCO SHEDS

245. A powerful line-up at Polmadie MPD, Glasgow, at around 9.00 p.m. on Friday 24 June 1960, with Coronation pacifics Nos. 46246 CITY OF MANCHESTER and 46224 PRINCESS ALEXANDRA, together with Jubilee No. 45717 DAUNTLESS, being prepared to work the overnight sleeping car trains from Glasgow (Central). (*W. A. C. Smith*)

246 (opposite above). A photograph at Carlisle Kingmoor that really puts size into perspective when you compare the locomotive to the size of its driver who is operating the water column at the shed on Saturday 31 May 1952. Fresh from works after overhaul, spotless Stanier Coronation pacific No. 46232 DUCHESS OF MONTROSE receives final preparations before the locomotive proceeds to Carlisle Citadel station to take over the down 'Royal Scot' from its southern counterpart. Between the tracks can be seen some of the many snowploughs that were stored at the shed. (*B. K. B. Green – Initial Photographs*)

247 (right). Another view at Carlisle Kingmoor in August 1964 finds BR Standard Clan pacific No. 72009 CLAN STEWART receiving maintenance to the inner workings of its smokebox, watched over by its shedmate Fowler Jinty 0-6-0 No. 47641. The smoke haze of a busy shed hangs heavy in the air on this sultry summer evening.
(J. G. Walmesley – The Transport Treasury)

248 (above). Looking quite resplendent in Highland Railway lined livery which at this time would have been olive green edged with dark green and black and white lines – dark red underframes and a vermilion panelled buffer beam, the first of Peter Drummond's Castle class 4-6-0s No. 140 TAYMOUTH CASTLE built in 1900 complete with double-bogie tender stands on the turntable at Inverness shed when nearly new. At this time the table was completely boarded out over the pit area and the shed entrance roads were fitted with double doors. (*Locomotive Publishing Company*)

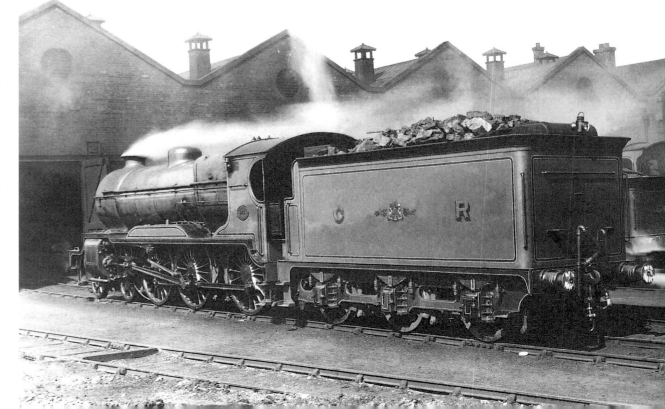

250. Owing to the shortage of motive power on the Highland Railway during the First World War, three more of Loch class 4-4-0s were built in 1917, a full twenty years after the remainder of the class entered traffic. One of the 1917-built locomotives which were fitted with Westinghouse as well as vacuum brakes No. 14396 LOCH RUTHVEN takes on water at Inverness on Friday 18 May 1928. Adjacent to the coaling stage, Fowler 4F 0-6-0 No. 4316 waits to be coaled up. This was carried out manually until the new mechanical coaling plant was constructed in 1930.   (H. C. Casserley)

249 (opposite below). One of F. G. Smith's controversial River Class 4-6-0s raises steam at Carlisle Kingmoor shed. They were built for the Highland Railway, but according to the Chief Engineer were too heavy to travel over Highland metals! This resulted in the complete class of six locomotives being sold directly to the Caledonian Railway. Considering these locomotives were built in 1915, they were very modern looking machines and from this angle could easily be taken as a forerunner of the Stanier 'Black 5s'. Looking quite resplendent in lined out Caledonian blue livery and numbered 943, the locomotive has "not to move" chalked on its tender buffers, suggesting that it had just been under repair.

251. An uncommon visitor to Stranraer builds up steam outside the shed on Saturday 18 August 1962 in the form of BR Clan pacific No. 72006 CLAN MACKENZIE which had worked a passenger train over the Port Road from Carlisle earlier in the day. Although they were infrequent visitors to the Port Road, the Clans appeared on a number of troop trains from Woodburn over the route just prior to the line's closure in June 1965.

(Ken Fairey)

252. The BR Standard Clan pacifics were well-proportioned machines as can be seen in this photograph at St Rollox shed of 72003 CLAN FRASER in pristine condition on Sunday 9 June 1957 having been in the works for overhaul. Half the class of ten locomotives were allocated to Glasgow Polmadie and the other half to Carlisle Kingmoor from where they worked for their entire existence. Much has been written, mostly critical, of the Clan's performance in service, but, with a footplate crew who knew how to get the best out of them, some excellent runs were achieved.

(W. S. Sellar)

253. This unusual picture was captured from the depths of Stirling South shed on Saturday 9 July 1966. Framed in the arched opening is the rather forlorn sight of Riddles ex-Ministry of Supply W.D. 2-8-0 No. 90370 from Wakefield shed. The locomotive appears to have suffered a mechanical problem as it stands outside as dead as a Dodo with the "not to be moved" baton fixed to the lamp bracket. The other arched opening perfectly frames the impressive signal gantry and signalbox behind which is the south end of Stirling station.

(Ken Fairey)

254 (right). A view looking from the shed across the turntable towards the entrance arch on Sunday 6 April 1958 finds a line-up of Stanier 'Black 5s', Nos. 44924, 45463 and 45492, all fitted with snowploughs. Nearest the camera is McIntosh 3F 0-6-0 tank No. 56262 above which can be seen the large mechanical coaling plant erected by the LMS in 1930. (*Neville Simms*)

255 (below). The grand central entrance, providing access to the turntable and the three-quarter segment roundhouse at Inverness shed was most imposing on Thursday, 31 July 1958, even though smoke and time had taken their toll of its structure. Perfectly framed in the arch, Stanier 'Black 5' No. 45453 eases off the turntable while preparing to leave the shed. (*Tony Heighton*)

256. The shed at Inverness is packed with locomotives in this early 1950s photograph taken from the coaling plant. The elevated viewpoint shows to good advantage the Doric style arched main entrance to the shed, a masonry structure which was in effect an elaborate water tower that really gave the depot an air of importance, which is of course it had, Inverness being the headquarters of the ex-Highland Railway. Designed by Joseph Mitchell, the shed was constructed in 1864 and stabled and serviced countless locomotives during the ninety-eight years until its closure in 1962. About to pass under the arch is ex-Caley 0-4-4 tank No. 55160 heading for the turntable. Adjacent to the 'Black 5' standing near the water column is the narrow gauge track on which the small hopper wagons could be manoeuvred to assist with ash disposal.

(P. L. Melvill)

257 (above). Located at the rear of the turntable, the small stone-built engine shed at Thurso was a sub shed of Wick (60D) and used to house the branch engine which on Wednesday 23 April 1952 was Small Ben Class 4-4-0 No. 54398 BEN ALDER. The locomotive is seen here taking an afternoon break from shunting the large amount of goods wagons on view, watched by railway employees during one of the quiet spells at the station. "Ben Alder" was built for the Highland Railway by Dubbs & Co. in 1898 and fitted with a Caledonian boiler in 1929. Still exceedingly smart in appearance at the time of this photograph, she was withdrawn the following February, but still languished at various locations for fourteen years, eventually being cut up in 1967, rendering the class extinct.

(H. C. Casserley)

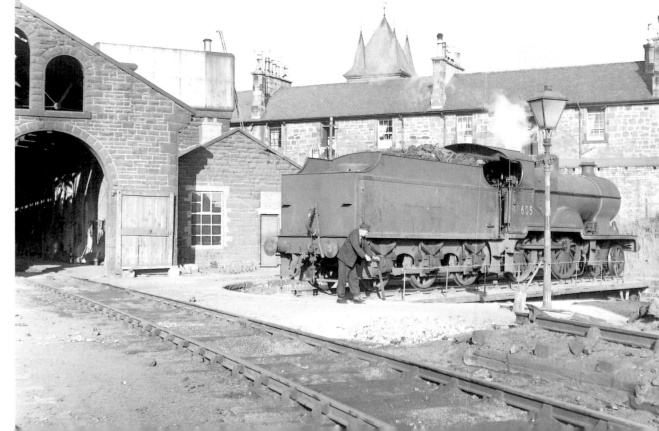

259. One of the large Pickersgill class 4P ex-Caledonian 4-6-2 tanks No. 15352 prepares to leave Polmadie shed after being serviced on Saturday 27 October 1945. Built in 1917 these tanks were mainly used for suburban passenger services but by 1950 the class of twelve was reduced to six all shedded at Beattock and used for banking purposes, the last member of the class being withdrawn in October 1953. In the background one of the sheds LMS 'Jinty' 0-6-0 tanks No. 7332 blows off excess steam while awaiting its next job. *(H. C. Casserley)*

258 (opposite below). On the evening of Saturday 16 July, during the long hot summer of 1955, class 2P No. 40605 is turned at Muirkirk, having arrived 8 minutes late at 7.02 p.m. with the two-coach 6.16 p.m. from Lanark for its return working at 7.15 p.m., the driver remarking that it was "all right" on the level, but that he preferred the Caley bogie (No. 54504) previously allocated to Muirkirk, The shed, which the G & SW had shared with the Caledonian, contained 0-6-0s Nos. 57236, 57573 and 57615, together with 0-4-4 tank No. 55264. *(W. A. C. Smith)*

260 (opposite). In the sunlight and shadowed interior of Ayr motive power depot stand the unmistakable shapes of Hughes 'Crab' 2-6-0s (or Horwich Moguls) the nearest being No. 42702. The Crab on the far side has the blower on to assist in the raising of steam pressure, pushing the smoke up into the roof void where it disperses through the smoke vents on the ridge, highlighting the shafts of light where the sun penetrates the smoke. These locomotives were two of the many Mogul 2-6-0s allocated to Ayr at this time where they were frequently seen working the area's coal trains. (*John Hunt*)

261. A sight to behold at Perth's Friarton depot on Thursday 2 August 1962 as the dazzling low evening sun highlights the red paintwork on Stanier Coronation pacific No. 46226 DUCHESS OF NORFOLK creating a dramatic image as the locomotive manoeuvres around the shed yard. Having been coaled and watered, it would soon be leaving for Perth General station to pick up an overnight sleeping car train to Euston, hauling it as far as Carlisle Citadel. Here the 'Duchess' would be replaced by another pacific for the remainder of the journey – 46226, driver and fireman returning to their home shed at Upperby and the end of another shift. (*R. A. F. Puryer*)

262 (left). On Tuesday 22 April 1952 a group of members of the Stephenson Locomotive Society requested that Clan Goods 4-6-0 No. 57956 be used to haul the 5.35 p.m. passenger train from Kyle of Lochalsh to Dingwall. Their request was granted and the locomotive hauled its last passenger train before being withdrawn from service the following month. Prior to working the trip we see the Clan Goods being coaled up by hand at the very basic coaling facilities that existed at Kyle of Lochalsh shed.

(H. C. Casserley)

264. In the grim surroundings of the coaling and ash disposal facilities at Greenock Ladyburn shed on Monday 9 July 1957, the depot's own locomotives, Fowler 2F 0-6-0 tank No. 47168 (this class was similar to the 'Jintys' but was fitted with smaller driving wheels and a shorter wheelbase for dock working) and ex-Caley 0-6-0 tank No. 56288 both receive attention. Ladyburn shed had half a dozen or more local trip and shunting turns identified by the target numbers, several being double shifted. Places covered included Regent Street Goods, Arthur Street Goods, Upper Greenock, James Watt Dock, Victoria Harbour, Port Glasgow, Bogston and Gourock. The dock lines were diagrammed for 0-4-0 saddle tanks (of which Ladyburn had two), the other turns being covered by "class 2 tank engines" of which there were five class 2F Caley dock shunters, two Fowler dock shunters and one Caley class 3F 0-6-0 tank. There was also a Caley 0-4-4 tank which acted as station pilot at Gourock. (*H. C. Casserley*)

263 (opposite below). This was a typical stage layout for manual coaling at a number of sheds in Scotland, this one being at 65D Dawsholm on Monday 15 August 1960 where local resident Fairburn 2-6-4 tank No. 42694 has its bunker topped up. Over to the right ex-Caley McIntosh 'Beetlecrusher' 0-6-0 tank No. 56168 busies itself shunting wagons. (*Ken Fairey*)

A RETURN TICKET TO SCOTLAND

265. To railway enthusiasts of the LMS system south of the border, the most widespread rumours revolved around spotting one of the fabled four Stanier 'Black 5' 'namers'. Graced with Scottish regimental names, they spent most of their existence based at sheds in Scotland. Here 45154 LANARKSHIRE YEOMANRY was not long out of works, standing at St Rollox shed on Sunday 13 July 1952. In later years 45154 and 45156 migrated south, being transferred to Newton Heath, Manchester. (*Ron Gammage*)

266. Lurking out of sight at the side of Ardrossan shed on Sunday 31 July 1955, Stanier 'Black 5' No. 45157 THE GLASGOW HIGHLANDER was in the process of being oiled up by the driver prior to its next job. This locomotive was the only one of the four to have the badge positioned above the nameplate. Along with 'Glasgow Yeomanry' it was shedded at St Rollox its entire working life. The adjacent stationary boiler appears to be set up to supply compressed air as well as steam for the shed facilities. (*Neville Simms*)

267. One of Ayr's resident Stanier 'Black 5s' No. 45460 prepares to leave the shed after having its steam worked up to full pressure by shed staff on an October day in 1964. The ex-G & SWR sheds at Ayr, Hurlford and Dumfries were very similar in design with their diminishing arched openings above the arched entrance roads except that Ayr was the same either end, being a drive-through shed. Steam depots were wet and dirty places but always possessed their own magical atmosphere.

(*Derek Cross*)

268. During the early 1960s when ex–LNER locomotives were hauling a number of services to and from Glasgow Buchanan Street, the ex-Caledonian shed at St Rollox occasionally resembled a London & North Eastern depot, as here on Easter Monday 30 March 1964. On view are class V2 2-6-0 No. 60816, A2 pacific No. 60527 SUN CHARIOT and A4 pacifics No. 60031 GOLDEN PLOVER and 60016 SILVER KING (whose footplate provided an ideal place to change a film). Also on view is local resident Standard class 5 Caprotti 4-6-0 No. 73146.   (*Neville Simms*)

269 (right). Inside Carlisle Kingmoor repair shop on Friday 29 May 1959, the coupling rods have been removed from BR Clan pacific No. 72009 CLAN STEWART. At the front end, fitters discuss their next plan of action in order to get the Clan back into traffic as soon as possible. On the plus side the BR Standard locomotives were supposed to have been designed with ease of maintenance a prerequisite. (R. C. Riley)

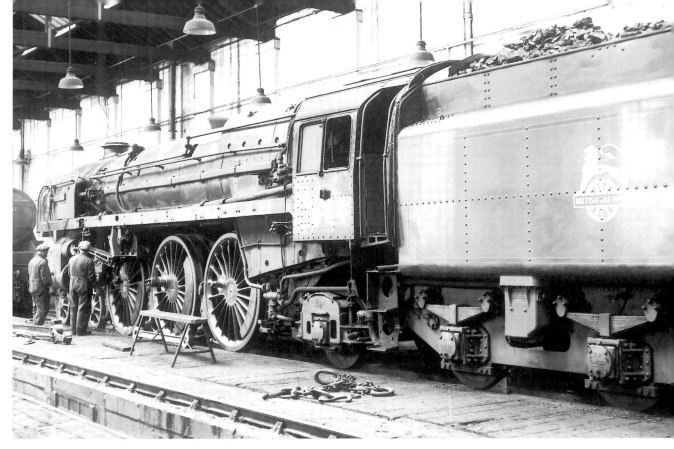

270 (below). In the works yard at St Rollox on Tuesday 21 June 1949 locomotives are prepared ready for work to be carried out on them against a backdrop of driving wheel tyres. The smokebox number plates have been removed and replaced by small markers with the locomotive number on. The existing painted number on Inverness 'Black 5' No. 45192 is unusually high up on the cab side sheet. Also waiting attention are McIntosh 3F 0-6-0 tank No. 16295 and a Fowler 4F 0-6-0. (H. C. Casserley)

271. It was good to find this impressive line up of ex-Highland Railway locomotives at Aviemore Shed especially as late as Tuesday 9 April 1946, and all in steam as well. On the left Small Ben 4-4-0 No. 14398 BEN ALDER stands alongside Loch class 4-4-0 No. 14379 LOCH INSH which has been rebuilt with a larger Caledonian boiler and Castle class 4-6-0 No. 14690 DALCROSS CASTLE. A wonderful sight, all gently simmering outside the shed as they bask in the spring sunshine during their twilight years.

(*H. C. Casserley*)

272. The light filters through the gloom inside Inverness three-quarter segment roundhouse shed on Friday 18 May 1928 revealing a classic ex-Highland Railway locomotive at this time looking quite resplendent in LMS red livery which suited them well. David Jones Loch class 4-4-0 No. 14383 LOCH AN DORB built in 1896 has been fitted with the Manson automatic tablet-catching apparatus on the cabside, the arm of which was pushed down into the horizontal position for the exchange of tablets while working single line sections of track.

(*H. C. Casserley*)

273. Gently simmering alongside Blair Atholl shed, Loch class 4–4–0 No. 14384 LOCH LAGGAN is serviced in this rural setting on Tuesday 15 May 1928. This member of the class had been sent to Hawthorn Leslie at Newcastle for a heavy overhaul, and came back with a new boiler fitted with Ross 'pop' safety valves and the louvered chimney shortened. Blair Atholl was a sub shed of Perth and locomotives working the local traffic between the two places were serviced there, but its main use was for stabling engines that gave banking assistance to northbound trains on the climb to Druimuachdar (Drumochter) Summit.

(*H. C. Casserley*)

274. Dugald Drummond-designed ex-Caledonian 0-4-4 tank No. 15103 is serviced outside the diminutive locomotive shed at Loch Tay, terminus of the Killin Branch on Tuesday 28 July 1931, prior to working the 1.20 p.m. train to Killin Junction. Although the Caledonian Railway provided the locomotives and rolling stock, the Killin branch was privately owned from 1889 until the LMS acquired it in 1923. (*H. C. Casserley*)

275. On Thursday 30 July 1931, the photographer travelled from Elvanfoot over the branch to Leadhills and Wanlockhead and while he was there visited the site of the Wanlockhead Mining Co. and found this diminutive Andrew Barclay 0-4-0 welltank (works No. 1790) built in 1923 and named WANLOCK working the system. The 1'-8" gauge railway was used for hauling hoppers of lead ore from the mine. (*H. C. Casserley*)

THROUGH THE LANDSCAPE

276. After a brief period of activity, peace and tranquillity descends again at Ballinluig station as Fairburn 2-6-4 tank No. 42168 recedes into the distance towards Pitlochry with the 9.25 a.m. train from Perth to Blair Atholl on Friday 12 July 1957. The down platform at Ballinluig was divided by the single gate level crossing; opposite the stranded section of the platform are the small goods facilities. Mainly a junction station, Ballinluig was closed to passengers at the same time as the Aberfeldy branch which it served, on 3 May 1965.

(*H. C. Casserley*)

277. Storm clouds gather over the impressive Nairn Viaduct at Culloden as one of William Stanier's 'Black 5' 4-6-0s heads its passengers towards Inverness after the long run down from Slochd summit on Thursday 5 August 1937. Built of red sandstone from local quarries, this is the largest masonry viaduct in Scotland. The main arch over the River Nairn has a 100 foot span; the remaining 28 arches have 50-foot spans, which in total carry the viaduct almost the full width of the deep green valley and at it deepest point is 130 feet from the track level to the river. The viaduct along with the line from Daviot to Milburn Junction at Inverness was opened for traffic in November 1898.

(*Les Hanson*)

278. Words seem almost superfluous to describe a scene as beautiful as this image set amongst the Trossachs on the Callander & Oban Railway as Stanier 'Black 5' No. 45099 drifts by with its train from Oban to Glasgow Buchanan Street on Tuesday 6 August 1957. Having skirted Loch Lubnaig and threaded the Pass of Lenny, the train is approaching the Falls of Lenny around a mile out from Callander. Sadly no trains travel along this way anymore, the section of line between Callander and Crianlarich having been closed on 28 September 1965.

(*W. S. Sellar*)

279 (above). The 'Beavertail' observation cars were originally built as part of the prestigious streamlined LNER 'Coronation' train which ran between Kings Cross and Edinburgh Waverley. When the service was discontinued, both the observation cars eventually found their way onto the West Highland and Callander & Oban lines, enabling passengers to admire the stunning landscape in luxury for an extra fare. Here one is seen bringing up the rear of the 5.15 p.m. train from Oban to Glasgow, hauled by a pair of 'Black 5s', passing the spur to Crianlarich Upper on Saturday 20 July 1957. The viaduct in the background carries the West Highland line over the River Fillan.   (*W.A.C. Smith*)

280 (right). The 'Beavertail' observation cars had the rear part of their bodies reshaped and insides refurbished at Cowlairs Works during 1959, as seen here near Loch Eilt on the Mallaig extension, Friday 9 July 1965. Both have been preserved.   (*Michael Mensing*)

281. Stunning views can be observed from the hills around Oban, unfortunately no longer ones like this superb panorama of the shed and goods sidings area, photographed on Sunday 12 June 1927. Adjacent to the locomotive shed are ex-Caley 'Jumbo' 0-6-0 No. 757 and ex-Caley 55 class Oban Bogie 4-6-0 No. 14607. These locomotives have been serviced after bringing in an excursion from Glasgow earlier in the day. In the siding a Pickersgill 191 class 4-6-0 builds up steam at the head of a rake of coaches while another 55 class 4-6-0 locomotive No. 14608 stands at the rear of the turntable pit. Towards the top of the picture on the left-hand side the roof of the station can be seen.

(*H. C. Casserley*)

282. The hills around Oban provided a good vantage point to obtain elevated views of the railways in the area. This particular panorama was photographed from McCaig's tower (seen on illustration 139) during the days of diesel traction on Wednesday 24 May 1972 but shows well the station frontage and overall roof, the carriage shed and railway pier.

(John Edgington)

283 (above). Twenty-four hours of torrential rain caused a landslide at Pinwherry which the midnight goods from Glasgow to Stranraer ran into on Wednesday 12 September 1962. The breakdown train was sent from Hurlford and here we see it after the recovery operation leaving Pinmore, hauled by 4F 0-6-0 No. 44281 with the re-railed wagons in tow. *(Derek Cross)*

284 (opposite above). The rolling Scottish south-west lowlands provide a pastoral setting around half a mile east of Dalbeattie on the ex-G & SW line between Dumfries and Castle Douglas on Monday 8 July 1963. Through this landscape came the rather unusual sight of ex-Caledonian McIntosh 3F 0-6-0 No. 57600 propelling its permanent way train back towards Dumfries. *(Michael Mensing)*

285 (opposite below). Making steady progress through the countryside, the 2.50 p.m. train from Dumfries to Kirkcudbright leaves the bridge spanning the Urr Water north-west of Dalbeattie on Sunday 13 July 1963. The train make-up is BR Standard class 4 2-6-0 No. 76073, a Southern region Combination Carriage Truck, an ex-works Stanier 57-foot Brake Third, and a Stanier 62-foot composite (both period 3). *(Michael Mensing)*

286 (above). On Wednesday 21 April 1965 north-west of Dalbeattie it appears to be the case of a "sledgehammer to crack a nut" as the very lightly loaded 8.07 a.m. combined train from Dumfries to Stranraer and Kirkcudbright bowls along behind a Stanier 'Black 5' and a BR Standard class 4 4-6-0. Having just crossed the bridge spanning the Urr Water the train 'such as it is' would be split at Castle Douglas.　　　(*J. C. Beckett*)

287 (right). The River Dee flows under the impressive Tongland railway bridge and the adjacent castellated road bridge from where it will turn into the estuary towards the sea and Kirkcudbright. Rumbling over the plate girder bridge on Thursday 11 July 1963 B.R. Standard 2-6-4 tank No. 80023 works the 9.30 a.m. train from Kirkcudbright to Castle Douglas. Passenger services ceased on this route in May 1965.　　　(*Michael Mensing*)

288. In classic West Highlands scenery, BR Standard 2-6-4 tank No. 80028 works away from Killin towards Killin Junction over the tumbling River Dochart during the last month of operation, September 1965. The coach is a Gresley steel-panelled Brake 3rd, deployed on the line because of its larger than normal battery capacity. The arches of the bridge were constructed in the summer of 1885 with the early use of concrete, each arch built up in layers to a depth of two feet, the piers and upper structure being masonry.

(*W. J. V. Anderson – Rail Archive Stephenson*)

289. After piloting an up train from Aviemore, Loch class 4-4-0 No. 14393 LOCH LAOGHAL stands at Dalnaspidal waiting to return from whence it came on Tuesday 15 May 1928, the Grampian mountains and Loch Garry form the background. Shortly after, the photographer was heading along the road to Druimuachdar (Drumochter) Summit to obtain further photographs when the driver of Loch Laoghal kindly stopped and gave him a lift on the footplate to his destination.

(*H. C. Casserley*)

290. An unusual view looking across Kyle of Lochalsh station and over Loch Alsh to the Red Hills on the Isle of Skye finds Clan goods 4-6-0 No. 17956 brewing up at the platform edge on Saturday 18 June 1937. The large building on the lochside was originally Lochalsh House, purchased by the Highland railway in 1896, when it became the Station Hotel. Refurbished and extended by the LMS in the 1930s as Lochalsh Hotel, it was sold off by British Railways in 1983. In the station yard, the lone Southern railway covered goods van is a long way from home territory. (*H. C. Casserley*)

291. Amongst typical Western Highland scenery the permanent way gang take a rest from their labours as Stanier 'Black 5' No. 45159 eases the 9.30 a.m. Oban to Glasgow Buchanan Street train away from Taynuilt station on Tuesday 17 May 1960. The gangers took great pride in the sections of track they were responsible for and competed with other gangs for the award of the "Prize Length". The tall lattice post lower quadrant signal dominates the view, and with its finial cap missing looks somewhat incomplete.

(*Michael Mensing*)

292 (above). A fine overall view of the branch terminus at Ballachulish on Wednesday 13 June 1956 finds 0-4-4 tank No. 55215 in the process of wasting steam while awaiting its 3.48 p.m. departure time with a train for Oban. The unsightly scar on the hillside behind is the result of quarrying for slate. To the left of the Station Master's house are the goods yard, crane and small wooden locomotive shed which was a sub shed of Oban. There was also a locomotive turntable adjacent to the shed.

(*John Edgington*)

293 (right). A mile or so east of Connel Ferry along the shore of Loch Etive, Stanier 'Black 5' No. 45163 drifts by with a down fitted goods of Presflo Alumina wagons bound for the British Aluminium Works at Kinlochleven on Tuesday 24 May 1960. Dominating the scene is Connel Ferry Bridge that carried the 27¾ mile long branch line over Loch Etive towards Ballachulish opened in August 1903.

(*Michael Mensing*)

294. Having breasted Druimuachdar (Drumochter) Summit 1484 feet above sea level on Tuesday 15 July 1952, double headed 'Black 5s' Nos. 45492 and 45461 have eased off as they start the downhill run towards Dalwhinnie and their eventual destination of Inverness with their train from Glasgow. As the noise of the train receded into the distance and the wind could be heard whining in the telegraph wires, there was an overwhelming feeling of remoteness in this wild landscape. This section of line was made single track during July 1966 but was doubled again in April 1978. (*Ron Gammage*)

295. A railway employee walks down the drive towards the station as the connecting bus to Aberfeldy sets out on its journey. Such was the familiar scene at Killin on Friday 20 August 1965. Over at the station B.R. Standard 2-6-4 tank No. 80126 simmers at the head of a train to Killin Junction 4¼ miles away. This rail service that had continued in a similar fashion for the past seventy-nine years would cease on 28 September and a way of life at Killin was changed forever.

(*John Hunt*)

225

296. Mid-winter in Scotland and steam in the landscape. A4 pacific No. 60009 UNION OF SOUTH AFRICA climbs the long Kinbuck Bank north of Dunblane with an excursion from Glasgow to Perth on Saturday 14 January 1984. Weather conditions on this day were particularly severe and after heavy overnight snow further blizzards driven on by a gale force wind made railway photography a real ordeal. At the time the train was actually due, the railway line in this picture was almost obliterated as snow was falling heavily. Running almost 3 hours late the train finally came as the sun was beginning to make an appearance for the first time in the day, although by now the photographer felt as though he was suffering from severe frostbite and had nearly given up sometime earlier! For once the long endurance test to survive the freezing conditions for a rare photographic combination of steam and snow proved successful on this occasion.

(*Joe Rajczonek*)

297. On an early morning in May 1963, Derek Cross waited with his camera at Crawick Water in Upper Nithsdale, about one mile north of Sanquhar; the setting and light were just right – all it needed was a train! After a while Stanier 'Black 5' 4-6-0 No. 44943 duly obliged heading across the viaduct with a northbound goods from Carlisle Kingmoor Yard laying a trail of exhaust in the still air, and the panorama was complete. (*Derek Cross*)

298 (left). The waters of the upper reaches of the Firth of Forth are dead calm in this photograph giving a perfect reflection of the ex-Caledonian swing bridge as a Thompson B1 4–6–0 rumbles over with its train heading north towards Alloa in the mid-1950s. After closure the bridge was eventually demolished and all that remains are the cut-off piers projecting above the water level.   (*P. Hay*)

299 (below). On the 'other' Forth Bridge, latterly used only by the Larbert to Alloa local service, is seen on Saturday 27 January 1968 with Park Royal railbus No. M79971 crossing on the 12.30 p.m. run from Alloa. Later that afternoon, the swing span was opened for an SRPS visit. It was operated by a steam engine dating back to 1885 with construction by the Caledonian Railway of the extension from the South Alloa branch and saw occasional operation for boats going up river to Bandeath naval stores depot. Closure of the Larbert to Alloa line, together with the associated Grangemouth branch, on 27 January 1968 brought to an end railbus operation by British Railways.   (*W.A.C. Smith*)

300. Connell Ferry Bridge is an impressive structure from whichever way you look at it, spanning the sea-loch of Etive which runs some distance into the mountains from its mouth at Connel. Near the bridge where the loch narrows there is a rock bar across and the water is shallow. Over the bar the water ebbs and flows in a four feet deep cataract and is called the 'Falls of Laura', the roar of which can be heard from afar at Spring tides. Here 0-4-4 tank No. 55238 works across the bridge with the 12.30 p.m. train from Connel Ferry to Ballachulish on Saturday 21 May 1960. The line to Oban passes in the foreground.

(Michael Mensing)

301 (left). With low cloud hanging over the pier and hills, BR Standard tank No. 80122 runs down towards Port Glasgow with the 3.30 p.m. from Wemyss Bay on Saturday 26 February 1966. The scene is dominated by the Clyde-built Cunard liner 'Queen Elizabeth' under refit in dry dock. Two years later she was sold to American owners for conversion to a floating university, but was destroyed by fire in Hong Kong harbour in early 1972. The photograph was taken on the last day of steam working on the branch before removal of running round and watering facilities at the 'Bay', DMUs then working the service pending electrification in 1967.

(W.A.C. Smith)

303. The 9.30 a.m. from Oban to Glasgow Buchanan Street heads through the Pass of Brander on the approach to Awe crossing on Monday 15 May 1961. The line through the Pass was protected by a system of wires and posts in an effort to stop boulders rolling down the mountainside and fouling the track. If the wires were broken the 'stone' signals would go to danger thus alerting the locomotive crew to proceed with extreme caution. In this view the wires and posts can be seen on the mountainside to the left of the track while ahead is one of the double-sided stone signals that were set at intervals along the Pass so that one was always in view of the driver. Down at water level, work proceeds on a Hydro-electrical scheme. *(Michael Mensing)*

302 (opposite below). Although Henry Casserley's main interest was locomotives, fortunately for us when something unusual caught his eye he could not resist the challenge of capturing the image on film, one example of which is this very moody scene across the water to Stranraer Harbour station at dusk on Monday 21 June 1937. The setting sun creates the unusual lighting effect on the small clouds while below, mostly in silhouette, the boat that plied across the Irish Sea between Larne and Stranraer is tied up at the dock. In the station, creating plenty of smoke and steam, LMS 2P 4-4-0 No. 646 and Hughes Mogul 2-6-0 No. 2918 are waiting to leave with the 9.55 p.m. Boat Train to Euston, known affectionately to local railwaymen as the 'Port Road Paddy' (see also title page). *(H. C. Casserley)*

A RETURN TICKET TO SCOTLAND

After an absence of 20 years, steam, in the form of 'Black 5' No. 5025, finally returned to the former Highland Railway line from Inverness to the Kyle of Lochalsh in 1982. On 29 May, 5025 hauled the very first train, a private charter for the Scottish Chamber Orchestra followed by a further series of private charters during early June, but the first public excursion ran on Saturday 25 September and was named the 'The Raven's Rock Express'. 'Black 5' No. 5025 spent part of its life working in Scotland and was fortunately saved from the cutter's torch and preserved by enthusiasts from the Strathspey Railway.

304. In this atmospheric landscape view looking across the townscape of Inverness, No. 5025 crosses the River Ness at low tide with the 11.25 a.m. departure on 25 September. A smoke haze lingers over the buildings with many church steeples prominent, whilst in the background the mountain range, called 'The Aird', overlooks the town. In this nostalgic scene it is difficult to believe that the sight of steam trains ever disappeared at all! (*Joe Rajczonek*)

305 (above). Immediately on leaving Oban, footplate crews faced the daunting task of lifting their trains up the 2½ mile climb to Glencruitten Crossing on a 1 in 50 gradient. From the photographer's bedroom window the 6.00 a.m. goods bound for Stirling is seen making a vigorous climb away from Oban on Thursday 9 August 1962, hauled by Stanier 'Black 5' No. 45214. At this time, the 6.00 a.m. goods and its balancing turn were the only steam workings on the Oban line (Monday to Friday). Steam assisted some of the diesel workings on Saturdays. *(Neville Simms)*

306 (below). On the evening of Sunday 12 June 1927, ex-Caley 'Jumbo' 0-6-0 No. 757 and ex-Caley 4-6-0 No. 14607 leave a drifting black smoke haze as they pound towards Glencruitten summit, returning their passengers to Glasgow. The families had spent the day sampling the delights of Oban, taking advantage of a cheap day excursion. *(H. C. Casserley)*

307. Between Crianlarich and Tyndrum, the railways of the 'West Highland' and 'Callander & Oban' run parallel to one another on opposite sides of Strath Fillan. On Monday 15 August 1960, photographed from a train on the West Highland line travelling towards Fort William, a goods train on the Callander & Oban is dwarfed by the landscape as it drifts eastwards towards Crianlarich Lower behind a Stanier 'Black 5' in the early evening. (*Ken Fairey*)

308. While climbing the steep gradient between Balquhidder and Glen Ogle summit on the Callander & Oban railway, a magnificent vista opens out on the right hand side across to Lochearnhead and down Loch Earn. In this wonderful view taken from the train on Saturday 2 June 1951, the railway line to Crieff winds its way through the landscape way below with Pickersgill class 3P 4-4-0 No. 54476 easing the 2.25 p.m. train from Balquhidder over the gracefully curved concrete viaduct.

(*H. C. Casserley*)

309. In the Highlands of Scotland the sheer size of mountain ranges and barren landscape are highlighted very effectively in this view looking towards Glen Carron mid-way between Inverness and the Kyle of Lochalsh on Saturday 25 September 1982. The River Bran on the left of the picture runs almost parallel to the single-track railway line as 'Black 5' No. 5025 is seen heading towards Achnasheen station, which is bathed in sunshine on the right hand side of the picture, with an excursion to the Kyle of Lochalsh. How small the train looks against the landscape. Fortune was on the side of the photographer on this occasion as the weather forecast suggested gales and heavy rain to which this part of Scotland is quite prone. But for once the sun stayed out to create a memorable timeless scene showing steam once again at work on this famous route.

(*Joe Rajczonek*)

310. A Scottish landscape of outstanding beauty greets the photographer looking across Loch Carron from Plockton on Saturday 25 September 1982. The trees of Strathallan Wood dominate the scene beneath the range of mountains with Duncraig Castle prominent to the left of the picture. 'Black 5' No. 5025 has just come into a clearing as it skirts the side of the loch with a train from Inverness to the Kyle of Lochalsh in this idyllic setting. Surely this line known as the 'Road to the Isles' must be one of the most scenic railway journeys in the British Isles, particularly memorable if one is steam–hauled!

(*Joe Rajczonek*)

INDEX OF LOCOMOTIVES
Numbers in italics are illustration numbers

Reid NBR 'Scott' D30 4-4-0
62418 THE PIRATE *138*

Gresley A4 (8P) 4-6-2
60009 UNION OF SOUTH AFRICA *296*
60016 SILVER KING *268*
60026 MILES BEEVOR *95, 96*
60031 GOLDEN PLOVER *268*

Gresley A3 (7P) 4-6-2
60057 ORMONDE *82*
60097 HUMORIST *41*
60100 SPEARMINT *81*

Peppercorn A2 (7P) 4-6-2
60527 SUN CHARIOT *268*

Gresley V2 (7P/6F) 2-6-2
60816 *268*

Thompson B1 5MT 4-6-0
61067 *115*
61244 STRANG STEEL *95*

Great Western Railway
Churchwood 'City' 4-4-0
3440 CITY OF TRURO *64*

British Railways
Riddles 'Britannia' 7P 4-6-2
70013 OLIVER CROMWELL *30, 36*
70027 RISING STAR *35*
70049 SOLWAY FIRTH *43*
70053 MORAY FIRTH *28, 46*

70054 DORNOCH FIRTH *28*

Riddles class 8P 4-6-2
71000 DUKE OF GLOUCESTER *7*

Riddles 'Clan' 6P 4-6-2
72000 CLAN BUCHANAN *198*
72002 CLAN CAMPBELL *104, 206*
72003 CLAN FRASER *252*
72006 CLAN MACKENZIE *251*
72007 CLAN MACKINTOSH *80*
72009 CLAN STEWART *49, 247, 269*

Riddles Standard 5MT 4-6-0
73055 *56*
73061 *216*
73099 *109*
73100 *156*
73104 *130*

Caprotti 73146 *268*
Caprotti 73152 *96*

Riddles Standard 4MT 4-6-0
75037 *36*

Riddles Standard 4MT 2-6-0
76002 *69*
76021 *164*
76073 *285*
76096 *130*
76101 *90*
76114 *77*

Riddles Standard 4 2-6-4T
80023 *287*

80026 *91*
80027 *54*
80028 *288*
80056 *61*
80093 *196*
80118 *142*
80122 *301*
80126 *295*

Riddles W.D. 8F 2-8-0
90370 *253*

Riddles W.D. 8F 2-10-0
90758 *179*

Diesel
N.B. Loco Diesel Electric
D6135 *139*

Park Royal railbus
M79971 *299*

Industrial
Andrew Barclay
ATLANTIC 0-6-2T 1907 *133, 134*
NCB No. 8 0-6-0T 1296/1912 *187, 188*
WANLOCK 0-4-0WT 1790/1923 *275*
0-4-0ST 1824/1924 *180*
NCB No. 6 0-4-0ST 2043/1937 *183*
NCB No. 17 0-4-0ST 2296/1952 *184, 185, 186*
NCB No. 25 0-6-0ST 2358/1954 *188*

Neilsen
JOHN BROWN and Co No. 2 4919/1896 *213*

311. Inverness shed on Friday 29 July 1955 viewed from above Milburn Road. (*Neville Simms*)